THE SIX

YOUNG READERS EDITION

THE SIX

YOUNG READERS EDITION

★ ★ ★ ★ ★ ★

THE UNTOLD STORY OF AMERICA'S FIRST WOMEN ASTRONAUTS

LOREN GRUSH

with *Rebecca Stefoff*

Simon & Schuster Books for Young Readers
NEW YORK   AMSTERDAM/ANTWERP   LONDON   TORONTO
SYDNEY   NEW DELHI

SIMON & SCHUSTER BOOKS FOR YOUNG READERS

An imprint of Simon & Schuster Children's Publishing Division

1230 Avenue of the Americas, New York, New York 10020

SIMON & SCHUSTER BOOKS FOR YOUNG READERS

and related marks are trademarks of Simon & Schuster, LLC.

For information about special discounts for bulk purchases, please contact

Simon & Schuster Special Sales at 1-866-506-1949 or

business@simonandschuster.com.

The Simon & Schuster Speakers Bureau can bring authors to your live event.

For more information or to book an event, contact

the Simon & Schuster Speakers Bureau at 1-866-248-3049 or

visit our website at www.simonspeakers.com.

Interior design by Hilary Zarycky

The text for this book was set in Adobe Garamond Pro.

Manufactured in the United States of America

0125 BVG

First Edition

2 4 6 8 10 9 7 5 3 1

CIP data for this book is available from the Library of Congress.

ISBN 9781534497047

ISBN 9781534497061 (ebook)

To the women who look up and dream of more

CONTENTS

CHAPTER ONE

A New World on Its Way

★ ★ ★ ★ ★ ★

One October night in 1957, a nine-year-old girl named Rhea followed her father out of their Tennessee home. He directed her gaze up toward the dark, toward a tiny blip of light zooming through the night. That moving dot in space was a satellite called Sputnik. Though it was no bigger than a beach ball, Sputnik was making history at that moment. It was the first object that humans had ever sent into orbit around planet Earth.

"You are watching the beginning of a new era," Rhea's father told her. "It's called the space age." Rhea suddenly understood that a new world was on its way, but she had no idea of the role space would play in her life.

Two years before that, hundreds of miles away in Oklahoma, a twelve-year-old girl named Shannon made a thrilling discovery. She'd been obsessed with space and the idea of traveling through it ever since picking up a science-fiction book in the library. Then, in 1955, she read in a newspaper article that *people* might soon be sent into space on rockets in real life. Shannon's excitement kicked into overdrive, and she decided to be part of that adventure. She'd found a way off the planet!

On a May morning in 1961, another nearly twelve-year-old girl, this one named Anna, sat on the dewy grass. She and her classmates were packed around a radio on the lawn of their school in Fort Campbell, on the Kentucky-Tennessee border. Her teacher had let them out of physical education class so they could listen to a fifteen-minute news broadcast.

That broadcast was the journey of Alan Shepard, the first American to travel into space. In Cape Canaveral, Florida, dressed in a silvery space suit and a white helmet, Shepard climbed into a capsule called *Freedom 7* that sat on top of a huge rocket. The rocket's engines fired, and it rose into the sky, launching the capsule into flight. At sixty-two miles above Earth's surface, *Freedom 7* crossed from the atmosphere into space. Before it splashed safely back down into the Atlantic Ocean, the capsule carried Shepard to one hundred sixteen miles above the surface.

Anna imagined it all as she drank in every scratchy word that came out of the little radio. "As he launched and I listened to him," she recalled years later, "I decided at that moment that, if I ever had a chance, that's what I wanted to do."

Rhea's Sputnik flight, Shannon's newspaper article, and the Shepard mission that Anna heard on the radio were not just inspiration for girls who dreamed of space. They were part of a contest between two world powers. This contest, the space race, was both scientific and political.

For almost half a century after World War II ended in 1945, the United States competed for global influence with the Soviet Union. (The Soviet Union was centered in Russia and included neighboring states that later became independent nations.) Many American citizens and political leaders saw the Soviet Union as their country's chief threat and rival. The Soviet Union and the United States never fought directly, but the decades of tension and conflict between them are known as the Cold War. The space race was one part of this war.

Both superpowers had learned during World War II that rockets had great importance in military operations. They also saw that rockets could advance the human presence into space. Neither superpower wanted to be outdone in scientific or technical achievements, and neither wanted the other to gain a military advantage by controlling space, so both the Soviet Union and the United States began to develop space programs. They planned to launch satellites, then probes and vessels with no crews, and eventually spacecraft that would carry travelers.

Sputnik, which Rhea saw from her yard as it crossed the night sky, was a Soviet satellite. While young Rhea gazed in wonder at the first human-made object to orbit

Earth, many Americans had a different reaction. The Soviet Union had beaten the US into space, which filled people with fear. In response the United States beefed up science education in American schools and pushed ahead its own space program. In 1958 the US government created the National Aeronautics and Space Administration (NASA) to run the program.

NASA called the people training for future space travel "astronauts," from Greek words meaning "star" and "sailor." The Soviets called their future space travelers "cosmonauts," or sailors of the universe. The Americans hoped to be the first to send a person into space, but the Soviets beat them there, too. Less than a month before Alan Shepard's short flight, Soviet cosmonaut Yuri Gagarin became the first person to orbit Earth. Not until early 1962 did an American astronaut, John Glenn, orbit the planet.

But the space race was far from over. It would continue over the next several decades while America's space program grew up—and so did the girls who dreamed of joining it.

Rhea, Shannon, and Anna were not the only ones with their eyes on the stars. A lawn in front of a California house became a space observatory for a science-loving girl named Sally after her parents gave her and her sister a small telescope. As a child Sally often set up the telescope for stargazing sessions under the night sky. She'd look at her favorite constellation, Orion, or the rings of Saturn. But like Rhea, Sally had no idea then that space would be part of her own future, or the important role she would play in the space race.

For two other young women, Judy and Kathy, the spark came later, but all six of these women shared a passionate drive to explore. They also shared a drive to stretch the limits of the possible, especially what people at the time believed was possible for women.

And they did stretch the limits. These six girls would grow up to become the first US women astronauts.

One of them would become the first American woman in space. Another would lose her life journeying there. One would become the first American woman to do a space walk; another would be the first mother to orbit Earth. Together all of the Six would make history not just high above Earth but on the ground. They would usher in another new era by breaking barriers, opening eyes, and showing the world what they could do.

CHAPTER TWO

Shannon: Fascinated by Flight

Even before Shannon had the strength to crawl, she knew life as constant motion.

Shannon Wells—later to become Shannon Lucid—was born in Shanghai, China, on January 14, 1943, as World War II was raging in Asia. Her parents were Americans: a missionary and the daughter of a missionary doctor.

Just six weeks after Shannon entered the world, though, her family was captured by the Japanese army, which had invaded China. They were placed in an internment camp, one of many places where Europeans and Americans who had been living in China were sent to live during Japan's occupation of the country. Although Shannon was too young to remember that time, the family lived in the camp for about a year before a Japanese ship took them to India on the first leg of a long trip that would return them to the United States.

The Wells family sailed around the globe twice as they made their way to the United States, including a stop in

South Africa, where Shannon received her first pair of shoes. But it was travel by air, not sea, that would eventually capture Shannon's imagination. After the war ended, the Wells family returned to China, and when Shannon was five, they took a journey that would have a powerful effect on her.

The family briefly moved to a mountain village to escape the summer heat of Shanghai. For the first part of the trip, they piled into a DC-3, an airplane left over from the war. Shannon's mother, brother, and sister all struggled to hold down their lunch in the turbulent air, but not Shannon. She peered out the window in awe as wispy clouds swirled around the mountain peaks.

As the plane came in for a landing on a tiny gravel runway, Shannon spotted a little speck on the ground. The speck grew bigger. She realized that it was a person, and that soon the family would be standing next to him.

"I saw this figure, this person standing down there with a red scarf around his neck, and I thought it was the most amazing thing in the world—that a human being, the pilot, will be able to get the airplane down there," Shannon later said. At that moment she decided that she would someday learn how to fly planes herself.

Shannon figured that this life in constant motion was how most families lived. But soon she would see for herself that this was not the case. The Communist Revolution swept across China, and the Wells family was expelled from the country. Back in the United States they settled for good in Bethany, Oklahoma, but Shannon couldn't quite accept their non-moving lifestyle. One day she asked her mother, "Why don't we ever go anywhere? Why are we just sitting here?"

"But it's wonderful!" her mother replied, much happier with her new life.

"No, it's not! I need to get moving!" said Shannon, who still had her eyes on the skies.

Luckily, Shannon soon found a new way to travel without leaving the house. In grade school she picked up her first science-fiction novel and escaped into the distant depths of the cosmos. She was hooked. She devoured tale after tale of spacefaring civilizations and heroes exploring the universe, and she'd start a new book as soon as the old one was finished.

It wasn't long before Shannon realized that space travel might be possible in real life, not just in science fiction. She learned of Robert Goddard, an early pioneer of rocketry, who had conducted rocket test flights in New Mexico. Shannon was inspired to build rockets of her own—models of them, that is. She'd "train" for space travel in the attic inside her own cardboard spaceship, one she was determined to fly all the way to Mars.

Spaceflight became an all-consuming passion. When her uncle visited from Michigan, she talked for hours about rockets and why the US should have a space program, until he asked, "Don't you talk about anything else?" But Shannon never let go of her love of space exploration, or her desperate desire to go into space.

At the age of twelve she read a newspaper article that suggested the Soviet Union would soon send humans to space. And not long after that, when she saw seven men on the cover of *Life* magazine, she learned that the United States was also launching its own space program, just as she had hoped. The *Life* article hailed those men as heroes and trailblazers. They were part of NASA's pioneering Project Mercury, a program to send the first Americans screeching beyond Earth's atmosphere into the void of space. That group, the Mercury Seven astronauts, would go on to achieve many of the United States' biggest milestones in human spaceflight.

But in spite of Shannon's excitement when she saw that magazine cover, she instantly noticed a trend. There was a John, an Alan, a Gus . . . but no Shannons. Only white men had been picked to be part of this elite spacefaring group. Her heart sank. She felt totally excluded.

Not content to accept this unfairness, she wrote to the magazine, asking its editors to explain why America was sending only men into space. She wanted to know if all Americans would ever be included. Surprisingly, she received a one-sentence reply from an editor.

"Someday, maybe females can go into space too," Shannon recalled the letter saying.

Getting to *someday* seemed to be taking a while, though, both in space exploration and in science on Earth, Shannon discovered.

By August 1963 she was close to graduating from the University of Oklahoma with a bachelor's degree in chemistry. It was time to start looking for a job, but she didn't know anyone who'd gotten a job related to chemistry. When she asked one of her professors for advice, he seemed stunned.

"What?" he asked, incredulous. "You're going to get a *job*?"

"Yes!" Shannon replied. "That's why I majored in chemistry."

Shaking his head, her teacher made his opinion clear. "There's absolutely *no one* who will hire you." He didn't spell it out, but Shannon understood what he meant. It was because she was a woman.

Shannon left the meeting shaken. But the hard truth was that her teacher was right.

After college she couldn't find any chemistry-oriented employers to give her a chance. The first job she managed to get was working the midnight shift in a retirement home—a far cry from the field of chemistry. "You just had to take up the crumbs that were left, that no one else wanted to do," Shannon would later say.

Eventually an opportunity opened up. A lab employee at the Oklahoma Medical Research Foundation left suddenly, and the nonprofit foundation was desperate to fill the position. Conveniently, there was Shannon, ready and willing to jump in. As a technician in the cancer research program, Shannon got her first taste of real lab work.

But although she loved working there, she noted that "discrimination was alive and real." There was no way for her to advance. And when she learned that funding for her job would end in two weeks, she had to act fast. Payments were due on a very important vehicle she owned, a Piper Clipper airplane.

After high school Shannon had followed through on the pledge she'd made back in China, when she'd seen that tiny man in the bright red scarf. She'd taken flying lessons, gotten her pilot's license, and eventually saved enough money to buy herself the little Clipper. She and her father flew in it together to church meetings. But to keep the plane in the air, Shannon had to find another source of income—fast.

She sent out resume after resume, yearning for a yes. Since "Shannon" wasn't a very common name back then, she'd sometimes get letters addressed to Mr. Shannon Wells. These were the nicer responses. One company asked her to send a picture of herself. When she did, she got a letter by express mail saying that the company had absolutely no jobs available. None.

"People weren't hiring women back in those days," Shannon later said. "And when I tried to get on with the federal government and their science labs, they wouldn't even look at a female."

Finally Shannon went to an employment agency in Oklahoma City and said that she was desperate. Did they have *anything* that'd be right for her? She was told that an employee at Kerr-McGee, an oil company based in the city, was leaving for six months for National Guard training. They needed someone to fill in while he was away.

Shannon happily accepted, even though she recognized unfairness in the situation. "I was coming in as a college graduate with some master's courses working in a job for somebody that I think was a college dropout." Still, she was grateful to have work that put her chemistry skills to use.

The six months at Kerr-McGee sped by. Just before Shannon's employment period was up, while she was again frantically searching for a job, one of her bosses told her that Kerr-McGee was open to hiring her full-time, but at a measly starting salary. This time Shannon spoke up. She said that she knew a coworker in the same lab was making much more than that, although he had less education.

Her boss just stared at her. "Shannon, you're a female. There's no way we're going to pay you the same that we're paying anybody else." Shannon didn't have much choice.

She'd be out of a job in two weeks. So once again she agreed to an unfair employment situation.

Then Shannon got an unexpected call. Mike Lucid, one of her former bosses, was inviting her to a boat show. His asking her out came as a bit of a shock. Shannon had absolutely no idea that he was interested in her, and besides, she had planned to take her plane out that same weekend. But bad weather prevented Shannon from flying, so she went to the boat show with Mike instead, and the pair started dating. When Mike eventually suggested marriage, though, Shannon told him there was no way that was going to happen.

"I plan to be a person—not someone's wife," she said. Many times during her childhood and career, Shannon had thirsted for adventure but had been held back or disappointed by a society that seemed intent on keeping her "in her place." She knew that married women were expected to stay home and do . . . something. "I never could figure out what people did at home," she said.

Like Shannon, Mike had grown up in the 1950s, when women's roles in society had been strictly limited. But also like Shannon, he didn't believe things had to be that way. At Kerr-McGee, Mike had originally thought the company was wrong to hire Shannon for just six months, as she was so overqualified for the job. He told her that if they married, she could work as much as she wanted. He'd fallen for the woman he'd met at Kerr-McGee, and he didn't want to marry a completely different person.

Shannon then confessed to Mike a secret desire, one she'd harbored since she was a little girl. She wanted to work for NASA someday—as an astronaut. What did he think about that?

"Absolutely, no problem."

So Michael and Shannon married in December 1967. But the joys of marriage were quickly overshadowed by the familiar sting of unemployment—at least for Shannon. When she became pregnant and told Kerr-McGee about it, her bosses immediately fired her.

Yet Kerr-McGee saw no reason to fire Mike, so for weeks Shannon stood at the door crying as he left each morning for work. Finally Mike suggested that Shannon go to graduate school to earn an advanced degree. In an unfair world her chances of long-term employment would be better if she gained as many credentials as possible.

So Shannon returned to the University of Oklahoma. She earned her master's degree in biochemistry and followed it with a PhD, also known as a doctorate, the highest degree awarded to graduate students. During that time she and Mike had their second daughter, but Shannon was back at school to take her finals less than a week after giving birth. "I couldn't put off the test," Shannon explained.

Even with a PhD, Shannon still struggled to find work.

After graduating, she suffered once again through months of job searches before she finally landed at a familiar place. The Oklahoma Medical Research Foundation took her on again in 1974, this time as a research assistant to study how various chemicals caused cancer in cells.

It was there that Shannon's biggest adventure would begin. One day in July 1976 she was in the lab, reading the foundation's science magazine, when she spotted a short article toward the back. It mentioned that NASA was recruiting a new round of astronauts for the agency's new space shuttle.

And this time the agency wanted women to apply.

Shannon had shared with Mike her dream of becoming an astronaut. Could it come true?

CHAPTER THREE

Rhea: Going Her Own Way

★ ★ ★ ★ ★ ★

Well before Rhea traveled to space, she traveled beyond everyone's expectations—including her own—to make her life into something extraordinary and challenging.

Margaret Seddon, who went by her middle name, Rhea, was born on November 8, 1947, in the upper-middle-class suburban town of Murfreesboro, Tennessee. She grew into a small girl with straight blond hair whose life at first followed the standard recipe for How to Make a Proper Southern Lady. She took ballet lessons. She learned formal dining etiquette. She played the piano, sewed buttons onto dresses, and planted herbs. Rhea's mother had learned these skills in her own youth. Now she was molding Rhea into the only type of girl she knew how to make.

"People always followed in their parents' footsteps," Rhea said later, "and I always thought I would be like my mother—be a Southern belle and stay home and cook and raise babies." But her father had other ideas. He wanted Rhea to have a bigger life than her mother and grandmother had known growing up. This meant exposing Rhea to a wider range of experiences. That's why, on that October night in 1957, he pulled Rhea outside and showed her the satellite Sputnik as it traced its historic path across the sky.

And it was the launch of Sputnik that ultimately led Rhea down a path different from the prim and proper one her mother had envisioned.

One of America's responses to Sputnik was to boost science education in grade schools. The nation hoped the next generation of youngsters would become brainiacs who could keep the US competitive in the space race. Rhea was one of many young students who fell in love with these science courses. She especially liked the life sciences.

Then college opened a whole new world to Rhea. She chose the University of California at Berkeley for its life sciences program. But when she arrived as a freshman in 1965, if felt like the school existed on another planet, not just in another state. The campus was bursting with political activism and had a population nearly three times the size of her conservative Tennessee town. During that first year her courses were tough, and Rhea struggled with her grades.

Then, the following summer, she got a taste of something new. Her father had been on the board of directors of a small hospital in her hometown. He arranged for Rhea to get a summer job there, and she ended up working in surgery. She was hooked from the start. By the time Rhea finished college, she was planning to become a surgeon.

She also planned to become a wife. A wedding date had even been set with her fiancé. But she would later say, "Came close to the time of the wedding, and I said, 'Not going to work.' He wants me to iron his shirts and stay at home and not go to work. So I backed out of the wedding."

It turned out to be the right decision. Marriage would have been the next step in the Proper Southern Lady life, but Rhea had found something else that she was passionate about. She kept her sights on a medical career and went on to enter medical school at the University of Tennessee. In her first year she was one of just six women in a class of more than one hundred. As she worked her way through the stages of becoming a doctor—medical school, internship, and residency—she got used to being surrounded by men.

When Rhea started her surgical internship at Baptist Memorial Hospital in Memphis, Tennessee, she wasn't permitted to enter the doctors' lounge, where physicians went to snatch some rest between performing surgeries. She was the only woman surgical intern at the time, and the lounge was for "men only." The head doctor said that this was because sometimes the men walked around in their underwear in the lounge. Rhea said that that didn't bother her, but he replied that the men would be embarrassed.

Instead, Rhea was told, she could wait between surgeries in the nurses' bathroom. Unable to change the policy, she took naps on a fold-out chair there, with her head resting against the wall. So when it was time for Rhea to begin her surgical residency, she moved to a hospital across the street rather than stay in a place with such sexist rules.

As a surgical resident in John Gaston Hospital's emergency room, she saw all manner of gruesome injuries. Emergency medical services crews would wheel victims of violence into the John, as the doctors called their hospital, and each night the emergency room had so many trauma patients that it earned an even more menacing nickname: the pit. The stitching that Rhea did there was far from the polite button stitching she'd learned as a child.

One morning, hours before the sun came up, Rhea was staring into the open abdomen of a patient on her operating table. She was trying to control the patient's blood flow while repairing the damage to his organs, caused by a bullet that had ripped through his stomach. She eventually stitched up her patient and sent him off to the intensive care unit. But while this operation had gone well and Rhea had grown used to grisly sights in surgery, that morning when she headed to the doctors' lounge, she wondered if this was the life she really wanted. Sometimes she just couldn't repair the damage, and those moments were the most devastating.

At that moment another doctor, Russ, sat next to her. He seemed to be having the same doubts and questions as Rhea. The two friends sympathized with each other over their exhaustion.

Then he asked Rhea a question that many people ask themselves when their circumstances seem dim or difficult. "What would you do if you weren't doing this?"

Becoming a doctor had been Rhea's top goal, but she'd also had a hidden motive for going to medical school. Secretly she wondered if it might lead to a future in space. Watching Sputnik cross the sky had planted a seed. Rhea figured that one day there'd be space stations orbiting Earth, staffed with doctors. And perhaps she could be one of those doctors living in space! That tiny thought had stayed with her for years.

So Rhea answered Russ's question honestly. "I'd be an astronaut." It was perhaps the first time she'd ever said it aloud.

Russ surprised her by replying, "I used to work for NASA." He mentioned that he still kept in touch with his former coworkers in the space program.

Several weeks later Rhea was going through a typical day, opening human bodies and stitching them shut. At one point she and Russ passed each other in a hallway. He stopped her and said, "Hey, some friends of mine say they're taking applicants for the space shuttle program. I hear they have an affirmative action program!"

He hurried off without giving any more information. Rhea stood there stunned, a million questions running through her mind. Affirmative action programs in colleges and other institutions were aimed at removing barriers and creating opportunities for minorities and women. So did Russ's remark mean that women could now apply for the space program?

Becoming a doctor had been an unexpected goal for a girl from Rhea's background. Now she might have a chance to make an even more unexpected dream come true.

CHAPTER FOUR

Anna: Sharing a Dream

Anna's path to space was like Rhea's in some ways, but her early life was more like Shannon's, full of change and movement.

She was born Anna Lee Tingle on August 24, 1949, in New York. Her father was an army sergeant who had met her mother while he'd been stationed in Germany, and every time he was assigned to a new military base, the family would be uprooted. From the time she entered the world, Anna found herself in a new hometown every couple of years.

As a shy little girl who enjoyed doing her math homework each night, Anna struggled to make friends and to shape her identity amid this constant change. But after she sat on the lawn outside her school, listening to the broadcast of Alan Shepard's momentous flight to space in 1961, Anna finally knew what path she wanted to take. At the same time, though, she thought her dream of going to space would never be possible.

That's because, like Shannon, Anna had noticed that

only men had been selected to be astronauts. On top of that, astronauts had to have jet piloting experience, something you could get only by joining the US military. And women were not allowed to fly jets for the armed forces. The barriers seemed too big to break, so she kept this dream to herself.

When Anna turned thirteen, she was attending her thirteenth school, but it was then that she finally got a break from constant moving. Her family settled in San Pedro, California, and unlike Shannon, Anna was relieved to then spend ten years in one place, so she didn't have to learn the names of a whole new crop of classmates every couple of semesters.

Then, while Anna was in high school, she and a friend volunteered at Harbor General Hospital. They took on the task of developing X-ray photographs in the hospital's darkroom—a pretty important gig for two high school students in the late 1960s.

One day the two friends stood next to each other in the dark, flipping film and plunging the photographs into their processing chemicals. Perhaps it was the absence of light that made Anna feel comfortable sharing her deepest, impossible desire, but in that moment she confessed something she'd never told anyone: "I'd really like to be an astronaut someday."

The friend was shocked. Anna had never betrayed

a hint that she was harboring that dream. But Anna had thought about it since that day by the radio in junior high. Being an astronaut was the perfect combination of everything she enjoyed: it involved science, it was challenging, and it meant exploring the unknown.

Anna's dream of going to space, though, was soon pushed to the back of her mind once more as she focused on simply continuing her education. Anna's teachers didn't exactly encourage women to seek college degrees, and most of the young women in her school didn't dream of more school or full-time work. They'd been told most of their lives that they wouldn't need such things when they grew older. Still, Anna set her sights on higher education and became the first in her family to go to college. She applied to just one school, the University of California at Los Angeles, and was accepted. In fact, she had done so well on her SATs that UCLA gave her a scholarship.

Anna first chose math as her major, but she started to wonder what she would actually do with a degree in advanced mathematics, since she did not want to be a professor or devote her life to working on complex math problems. Chemistry classes also intrigued her, so she made the leap to a chemistry degree, figuring that she could do more with a science education.

Her time at UCLA was intense, and after a brief whirlwind romance, marriage, and divorce from a man who turned out not to be the right partner for her, Anna decided to apply to UCLA's medical school.

While Anna Lee, as she now called herself, loved the idea of a career as a doctor, she also had the same hidden motive as Rhea. Still dreaming of going to space one day, she too figured that eventually there'd be space stations orbiting Earth—and those stations would need doctors. Anna thought perhaps she could be one of the doctors living at those stations, attending to sick astronauts.

But UCLA reviewed Anna's application to medical school and put her on the university's waiting list. Despite the blow of not being immediately accepted, Anna made the most of that time. She earned her master's degree in chemistry while working as a teaching assistant, and that degree would come in handy in the years to come.

When Anna did get into medical school, she chose the familiar environment of Harbor General Hospital for her internship. And it was there that she met Bill Fisher, a surgical intern who was a year ahead of her. The two had quite a few things in common. Of course they shared a passion for medicine, but they learned on their first date that both of them had deep desires to become astronauts. They talked all the time about how, if the opportunity ever came up, they'd jump at the chance to apply to NASA. Bill proposed marriage less than a year after they met.

One day not long after Anna and Bill became engaged,

she was slumped down in a chair at Harbor General, completely exhausted. She was in the middle of another twelve-hour day at her surgical internship. The whole year after graduating from medical school had been like this: back-to-back shifts on her feet, last-minute surgeries at any wild hour of the night. She knew these were the dues she had to pay to become a surgical resident, but, again like Rhea, she'd started to wonder if this was really the life she wanted.

As she took a second to relax, she heard a familiar voice over the hospital's PA system. It was Bill, her fiancé, paging Anna to call him. *I wonder what this is about,* she thought.

Anna wrenched herself from her chair and made her way to a nearby phone. As soon as Bill answered, his excitement seemed to leap out of the phone's speaker. A friend had just shared a major piece of information. NASA was about to recruit a new round of astronauts, and this time women were encouraged to apply.

The deadline for applying was just three weeks away, but the news filled Anna with newfound energy. She'd been waiting for this moment ever since she was a little girl. And now she had the right scientific and medical credentials to give it a shot, as well as a partner who shared the same dream.

CHAPTER FIVE
Sally: Picking a Path

S ally loved gazing through her telescope at the stars when she was a girl, but she didn't initially dream of traveling to space the way Shannon, Rhea, and Anna did. Her dream led her down a different path—until she had to choose whether to stay on it.

Sally Ride was born in the Encino neighborhood of Los Angeles, in California's San Fernando Valley, on May 26, 1951, but she didn't spend her whole childhood there. In 1960 her parents took Sally and her sister on a yearlong road trip through Europe. It was an enlightening break from their former lives, full of new cultures and foods. And it was also the birth of a new passion. On a burnt-orange clay tennis court in Spain, Sally picked up a racket for the first time. She lit up that day.

When the Ride family returned to Encino in 1961, Sally threw herself into tennis. She took to the game with ease, having always been a skilled athlete and lover of sports. Baseball had been Sally's first love. As a California girl, she revered the Los Angeles Dodgers above all else, and when she was just five years old, her father taught her how to read and decode the team's box scores in the newspaper each morning. Perhaps that introduced her to math, which would play a big role in her future.

Tennis brought Sally many things, like dexterity and good hand-eye coordination. It also brought her a core group of friends who shared her love of the game. During one tournament she played against a twelve-year-old girl named Tam O'Shaughnessy. They instantly clicked. Tam's mother and Sally's father watched in frustration as the two girls spent more time gabbing with each other than trying to finish the match.

After that, Sally often traveled to San Diego, farther south on the California coast, to meet Tam and other tennis friends, or those friends would come to Los Angeles to see the Ride family. Together they'd practice their drop shots during the day. Then, if they listened to records later, a dance party might break out. Sally usually sat in the corner, not wanting to draw attention to herself, until Tam spied her and pulled her into the group. After that it wouldn't take long for Sally to start singing along with the rest.

Sally's tendency to hang back showed itself in tennis, too, but it wasn't a lack of courage. Sometimes she just wanted to be a little lazy. She'd often blow off her commitments so she could sprawl in front of a television screen. Her father would encourage her to get up to practice more, but Sally wouldn't budge. She valued her downtime as much as she valued achieving the perfect tennis shot.

Still, Sally became a powerful player. Her tennis skills eventually won her a place on the team at the ritzy Westlake School for Girls, attended by children of wealthy businesspeople and celebrities. Sally was a great student there, when she wanted to be. But just as she would sometimes blow off tennis practice, she'd often put off doing her homework. In fact, she sarcastically prided herself on being an underachiever. If Sally didn't like something, she wouldn't throw herself into it. This was especially true for English and history classes, where she dreaded being called on by her teachers.

Science classes were a different story.

Sally had gotten her first taste for science and space when she was young, after her parents had bought her that telescope. She'd peer through its glass at night, pinpointing the constellations and passing her fascination with the sky along to her friends. One of them later recalled, "We slept out on the lawn one night, and we're looking at the stars and we're talking about, you know, the enormousness of the universe and how many years it takes for light to get here. And her imagination was really captured by all of that."

What really sent Sally's passion for science into overdrive was one of her eleventh-grade teachers, Dr. Elizabeth

Mommaerts, who taught physiology, the science of how living things and their body parts work. Dr. Mommaerts had been a professor at UCLA, a rare woman with a PhD at the time. Plus she was just plain cool. Hungarian and cosmopolitan, she brought a college-level understanding of science to her high school students and hosted dinner parties for the best of them, including Sally.

Although not a particular fan of physiology, Sally admired Dr. Mommaerts and the way she taught, and cared a great deal about how her teacher saw her. Dr. Mommaerts saw Sally's potential and not only inspired her deep love of science but encouraged her to pursue a career in research, whatever kind it might be.

All these experiences led Sally to choose physics, the science of matter and energy, as her major when she headed to Pennsylvania's Swarthmore College on a full tennis scholarship in 1968. She loved the school, and the classes fed her growing love for physics. But she grew homesick for California, where the weather was much more favorable to outdoor sports. During her time in the Northeast, Sally dominated the tennis tournament circuit with an outrageous winning streak. She wondered, Could she succeed as a professional tennis player?

So Sally dropped out of Swarthmore after three semesters and went home to try. No more ditching practice when she didn't feel like it. It was time to buckle down. Once back in the Los Angeles area, she transferred to UCLA, joined the university's tennis team, and got to work. But after a few months of backbreaking tennis, Sally realized that despite her skill and all her victories, her heart just wasn't in it. She couldn't fully commit to the packed days of practice it would take to become a master.

She had also come to realize that science and education were much more important to her than tennis. She even started to appreciate her English classes! Up until then Sally had been walking two paths. One led to athletics. The other led to science. But the time had come to make a choice, and finally her decision was clear. She chose the path that led to further study and transferred to Stanford University, near San Francisco.

Sally truly loved Stanford, with its arched sandstone buildings nestled among the redwoods and rolling hills of Northern California, so after receiving her undergraduate degree, she stayed for graduate school, specializing in physics. She was one of just a handful of women in the physics department, but that didn't hold her back. When a professor told Sally that usually 60 percent of his students dropped out, she fought her fear and finished the semester, watching her fellow students disappear one by one.

After a few months Sally began focusing on astrophysics, the science of how celestial objects such as stars and planets form and interact throughout the universe. It was a natural extension of her childhood hobby, looking up at the night sky to trace the twinkling constellations. Now Sally was no longer a self-described underachiever. She put everything she had into her studies and loved doing research.

Life in grad school was good for Sally. She was happy to be living in her home state again. She thrived on her studies. And she had become part of a tight foursome that included fellow students Bill Colson and Richard Teets and her roommate, Molly Tyson. The group got together almost daily to play volleyball, often followed by dinner at Sally and Molly's tiny two-bedroom house on the Stanford campus.

One day, though, Bill sat down with Sally and told her that he'd developed feelings for her that were stronger than friendship. At that moment Sally had to make another choice—whether or not to share something important and private.

She was quiet for a minute. "This is really difficult," she finally said. After another pause she revealed why. "I'm in love with Molly."

It was the first time Sally had admitted that to anyone other than Molly. Until that point their romantic relationship had been conducted strictly behind the scenes. It had begun as friendship. After they'd met as kids on the junior tennis circuit, they'd reconnected at Stanford and quickly become inseparable. They did everything together, from weekend trips to writing a long silly children's book on butcher paper.

Then, during Sally's first year at Stanford, her boyfriend broke up with her and she suffered her first real heartbreak. Molly was there to comfort her. In time that comfort grew into a romance. For both it was their first relationship with another woman.

As such, they decided to keep it private. Attitudes toward same-sex relationships were changing in the 1970s, but there were still a fair number of people who disapproved of them. Also, both Molly and Sally had only dated men until then. Neither woman was ready to openly declare herself gay after one relationship. Their secrecy was so complete that Bill had never suspected anything. He took Sally's news in stride, though, and didn't judge her and Molly.

But Molly and Sally were nearing the end of their relationship. They'd been seeing each other in private for close to five years, and it had been a remarkable journey, but Molly was finding it hard to date someone who seemed almost godlike in some ways—a great athlete *and* a great scholar. Beyond that, Molly wanted to be more open. She was tired of living in the dark and was eager to shine a light on her true life with Sally.

Sally wasn't ready for the world to see her that way,

though, and their conflicting desires led them to break up. Molly moved to New York and became a sportswriter, leaving behind California and Sally, who found herself heartbroken once again. But she slowly moved on with her life at Stanford, and this time she pursued Bill. They became a couple.

In January 1977, with a year and a half to go at Stanford, Sally began thinking about what lay ahead after graduate school. She and Bill had talked about it. They figured that, upon graduation, they'd probably go off and become professors somewhere.

Then one morning a new path—and another choice—presented itself to Sally. She walked into the Stanford student union for breakfast before class. As she took a bite, she reached for a copy of the *Stanford Daily*. Her eyes lit up as she read the headline of an article on the first page:

NASA TO RECRUIT WOMEN.

CHAPTER SIX

Judy: Excellent at Everything

★ ★ ★ ★ ★ ★

With a brilliant, logical mind, Judy Resnik grew up a star at everything she did, but she yearned for something she could throw her whole self into. She just needed to find the right space in which to shine.

Born on April 5, 1949, in Akron, Ohio, Judy learned to read and solve math problems in her first five years of life. She was so advanced, in fact, that her kindergarten teacher recommended that Judy skip to first grade.

She was one of the youngest kids in her elementary school class, but schoolwork came easily to her—and it wasn't the only thing. Judy started taking piano lessons, and soon she flourished as a classical pianist. Her music teachers told her parents that she could play professionally someday.

From the beginning Judy's mother, Sarah, demanded excellence. Sarah tried to give Judy a sense of order and discipline by creating a very regimented life for her. Judy would come home from school to find a table covered with the ingredients to bake cookies. Sarah would hover over Judy, dictating how to put the ingredients together, walking her through the process step-by-step. After baking class it was time to hit the piano keys. Such lessons happened all the time, with Judy's life after school controlled down to the minute.

Judy had a much more relaxed, warmer relationship with her father, Marvin. A friend of Judy's recalled that when Marvin came home, the energy in the room would shift. "The minute he came home from work, the kids were freed and they'd go right on his leg," she said. "And he just spent an amazing amount of time with them." When company came over, Judy would immediately go to the piano to play, and Marvin would sing. He never skipped a chance to talk about how proud he was of her accomplishments.

Judy inherited traits from both Sarah and Marvin. She could be distant and intense, focused on her studies and work, but her friends also knew her as kind and compassionate. She didn't express her feelings much, but she was warm to the people she loved and available when someone close to her needed a hand.

As different as their parenting styles were, Sarah and Marvin were united in their disapproval of Judy's "bad boy" high school boyfriend, Len Nahmi. He was Judy's opposite in a lot of ways. He didn't make great grades, he wasn't a hard worker, and, unlike the Resnik family, he wasn't Jewish. When her parents told Judy that she wasn't allowed to see him, though, she still found ways to do so. Len might not have been the star that Judy was, but he wanted to fly planes one day, and that intrigued Judy.

At the same time, Judy's parents' marriage began to suffer, and so did Judy's relationship with her mom. "When Judy was fourteen, all her friends were ice skating," Marvin recalled once. "She asked for a pair of ice skates and Sarah said no. So I went out and bought her a pair. Sarah burned them. Can you imagine? Next year, I bought her another pair."

Adding to the level of friction, Sarah still didn't approve of Len, and the young couple grew tired of the immense work it took to stay together. Len finally broke up with Judy, telling her that "the whole thing was causing her nothing but anxiety and pain."

In spite of family and romantic turmoil, Judy continued to excel, achieving a GPA of 4.2 in high school. She was the only girl in her school's math club, a gender-unbalanced situation she'd encounter often in life. Her crowning achievement, though, was a perfect score on the math portion of her SATs. She graduated from high school at the top of her class.

Marvin and Sarah divorced when Judy was seventeen. As was usual at that time, Judy and her brother, Chuck, went to live with their mother. But before she left for college, Judy made a bold move for a teenager. With the help of her father, she prepared a court case, asking to have custody switched from her mother to her father. The court granted the request.

It was mostly a symbolic gesture. Soon Judy would be going off to Pittsburgh, Pennsylvania, for her freshman year at Carnegie Tech (now called Carnegie Institute of Technology). Still, Judy remained close with her father while she was in college, writing letters to him in Hebrew and bringing a new boyfriend to visit. Eventually Judy's dad remarried, giving her twin stepsisters she grew to adore.

Judy's new boyfriend was Michael Oldak, a smart, driven electrical engineering major. He recognized Judy's intelligence and wasn't intimidated by her brilliance. And he was Jewish, which pleased her extended Jewish family, including the grandfather who had been a rabbi in Russia.

When Judy began dating Michael, she accompanied him to a few of his classes and found she really enjoyed them. She wound up switching her major from math to electrical engineering. There were only two other women in the whole program, but Judy took to her new major with ease. While Michael would stay up all night studying for his exams, Judy would be in bed by ten, confident she had all the answers for the next day's tests. And she was usually right. She got top marks in all her courses. "She was just absolutely brilliant and extremely talented at anything she did," said Michael.

The couple bonded over more than schoolwork, though. While on a date to a theme park, Michael urged Judy to ride a roller coaster with him. At first she said no, but he finally wore her down, and they spent a heart-stopping three minutes whipping up and down the steel rails. Afterward she turned to him and said, "Let's go again."

Still, it was hard for people in Judy's life, even Michael, to truly know her. Although she remained close with her father, her relationship with her mother grew more strained. The emotional distance between Judy and Sarah widened during the Carnegie years, which may be one reason why Judy remained an intensely private person who kept to herself.

Right after graduation—Judy had again finished near the top of her class—she and Michael were married in the same synagogue where she'd been confirmed during high school. The newlyweds moved to an apartment in New Jersey, and both of them found jobs at the electronics and technology company RCA. Judy worked as a designer of integrated circuits. Although she was one of very few women engineers, the company recognized her formidable mind and even offered her a salary higher than Michael's.

After a couple of years at RCA, Michael decided to make a big change and go to law school at Georgetown University in Washington, DC. To stay with him Judy requested a transfer to RCA's offices in Springfield, Virginia. But just as Rhea and Anna had questioned whether the life of a surgeon was what they truly wanted, Judy began to wonder if her future really lay with RCA.

Ultimately Judy left the company for a research fellowship from the National Institutes of Health (NIH), which let her pursue her PhD in electrical engineering from the University of Maryland. While she studied, she took on the role of biomedical engineer at the NIH, using her logical mind to help doctors learn more about the structure of the human eye—and making her optometrist father proud.

The next years of study and focus were an intense time for the young couple. Judy spent hours upon hours in the laboratory, peering through a microscope at a frog's exposed retina. But she still questioned whether this was what she wanted to do for the rest of her life. Frustrated, she asked a coworker, "Where do you get your ideas from?" It was as if she were seeking the source of scientific inspiration, which had so far eluded her. He replied that if she had to think about where ideas come from, the research she was doing might not be the field for her.

Eventually Michael finished law school. With the future now visible to him, he talked to Judy about starting a family. But while there was much she was still figuring out about her own future, she'd known for years that she didn't want children, possibly because of her painful battles with her mother. Judy's firmness on this topic soon drove a wedge between her and Michael, who loved his wife but understood that her life was going in a direction different from his.

Their divorce was as friendly as one could hope for. Afterward Judy and Michael had good feelings toward each other and communicated whenever they achieved milestones or faced crises.

Judy stayed in Washington and put her energy into her studies and work, still searching for something to throw her whole self into. During her downtime she would visit the beach with friends. One day she even sent a postcard to Len Nahmi, who had followed through on his desire to fly planes and was working as a pilot for Air Canada in Toronto. She told him she was single, and he hopped onto a plane to DC, beginning a series of back-and-forth visits for the two. They never became a couple officially, but they were in each other's lives again.

And then one day in 1977, Judy found what she'd been searching for. She turned on the radio and heard an announcement about NASA's new astronaut selection. Or she saw an advertisement for it on a bulletin board at work. Or maybe she heard about the selection from Len, who'd heard about it on the radio in Toronto. Over the years various versions of the story have appeared.

But the key detail is that Judy heard the news. One day on the beach a friend asked Judy what she was doing, scribbling on a piece of paper. "Applying to be an astronaut," she said.

CHAPTER SEVEN

Kathy: From Sea to Space

★ ★ ★ ★ ★ ★

From as early as she could remember, Kathy wanted to explore the unknown. That drive would carry her to unexpected heights—and to the deepest depths imaginable.

Kathryn Sullivan was born in Paterson, New Jersey, on October 3, 1951. From the start it was in her nature to want to figure things out and unravel the mysteries of the world around her. When she was in kindergarten, she saw a television ad for a plastic toy gun, one that mimicked the movement of a real gun turret on the deck of a battleship, jerking back when it was fired. She had to have that toy. Not because she was developing a love of guns but so she could see how its levers made it work. She was already thinking like her father, who was an engineer.

Along with her interest in figuring out how things worked, Kathy also had the spirit of an explorer, but it was the planet she lived on, not space, that first fascinated her. Maps were her gateway to this passion. She devoured images of the intricate landscapes and riverbeds speckled across the European continent, and the vast mountain ranges and distant oceans of Asia.

By age seven Kathy had created her first map. She'd learned the language of mapmaking by decoding the legends and directions she'd seen on the maps in *National Geographic* magazines.

Kathy had also crossed the country—in person, not by studying a map. The family moved to Van Nuys, California, when her father, Donald, took a job as an aerospace engineer for the Marquardt Corporation. The company was involved in the development of the ramjet engine, a type of engine used in supersonic—faster-than-sound—flight. After that, planes became part of Sullivan family life. Donald would bring home schematics and blueprints that Kathy would trace with her fingers.

Marquardt's headquarters happened to sit right next to the Van Nuys Airport, and Donald soon joined the company's flying club. He took small planes such as Cessnas and Pipers into the air to join buddies on fishing trips. Kathy's brother, Grant, also caught the flying bug.

But Kathy was drawn to more earthbound travel and exploration. Travel of any sort would have to wait, though, because Kathy was needed at home. When she was twelve, her maternal grandmother and only living grandparent died of cancer. Stricken by grief, Kathy's mother turned to alcohol, and Kathy watched as her mother became crushed by depression.

Kathy soon found herself stepping up to help keep the family going. She took on household cleaning tasks and the role of peacemaker during tense fights. She and Grant would even disable the car when their dad was at work, hoping to keep their mother from getting behind the wheel after drinking.

Kathy yearned for a time machine so that she could travel back and retrieve the mother she had once known. Thankfully, Kathy's mother eventually sought therapy and emerged from her depression, though life was never quite the same again in the Sullivan household.

As Kathy approached the end of high school, she set a concrete goal for herself. She was going to live abroad. She figured that foreign languages would be her passport to such a life, so she decided to major in languages when she started college at the University of California at Santa Cruz.

The focus on languages didn't last long. During Kathy's freshman year an advisor insisted that she take three science classes. She didn't want to, but her advisor held firm. He even suggested classes she might enjoy, such as oceanography, the science of the oceans; and geology, the study of the physical structure of the earth.

Those classes introduced Kathy to a world she hadn't known existed. One of her professors would take students out to the tide pools along the California coast, looking for strange ocean critters such as sea squirts. Kathy found the rhythms of the tides and currents fascinating. She was captivated by the rocky structures stretching across the sea-floor and the ways that land and sea intertwined. She felt unexpected excitement when she learned that the people who studied the oceans got to explore the world—in fact, their jobs required it.

Kathy eventually mustered the courage to ask one of her oceanography teachers what the job of an ocean-ographer was like. He took her under his wing, patiently answering her questions and suggesting classes she could take. And a few courses later, Kathy made the switch from languages to earth sciences. The change still let her achieve her dream of living abroad, though. In her junior year she studied at the University of Bergen in Norway.

It was an exciting time to be a student of the oceans.

Just a few years before Kathy had entered college, geologists had begun to accept ideas once considered daring, or even outlandish. Those concepts—plate tectonics and continental drift—explained how the earth we know today was shaped by the extremely slow movement of gargantuan landmasses. Scientists now believe that, over millions of years, the continental landmasses drifted into their present positions, like puzzle pieces fitting together, and are still moving extremely slowly. This new understanding opened up a ton of research opportunities for young oceanographers. Kathy rode that wave in Norway, and later at Dalhousie

University in Nova Scotia, as she worked toward her PhD.

One day, after three and a half years at Dalhousie, Kathy stood on the deck of the university's white research vessel, speeding through the wide-open waters of the North Atlantic Ocean. She tasted the saltiness of the chilly ocean waves crashing against the side of the boat. The crew's focus of interest, though, was far below.

Kathy and her expedition team were headed to the Grand Banks, a submerged chain of plateaus off the coast of Newfoundland in Canada. Long-dormant volcanoes dotted the edges of these underwater plains. Kathy and her crew were going to investigate these ancient peaks.

Once the ship was positioned above one of the sunken summits, Kathy hoisted a cable overboard and dangled it under the surface of the water. The goal was to gently scrape the tops of these mountains, capturing a small sample of material to bring back home. Kathy and her team were eager to know what kinds of chemicals had been deposited in these old volcanic rocks. That information might provide a clue as to how the seafloor of the Atlantic Ocean had first formed.

For Kathy nothing could compare to being out at sea like this. She loved the thrill of a successful expedition. It felt like orchestrating a beautiful song. Most of all, this was the kind of adventure she had always dreamed of as a girl—standing out here on a boat surrounded by nothing but crystal-blue ocean, the northern wind whipping through her hair.

Although Kathy was having the adventure of a lifetime on the Atlantic's surface, what she really wanted was to dive below the surface of the ocean. On a previous expedition she'd been on a vessel that had held the *Alvin* submersible, a mini-submarine that can carry people down to extreme ocean depths in order for them to properly map the sea-floor. As soon as Kathy had seen two researchers descend in that submersible, she'd known that she wanted to one day pilot *Alvin* herself. Her goal was to travel as deep as she could below the ocean's surface.

When Kathy returned to California at Christmastime in 1976, she brought tales of her expeditions home with her and confided to her brother that she wanted to dive in *Alvin* someday. Grant listened to her talk about her goals, but then he suggested a different career path, one that would take her literally in the opposite direction. Had she considered applying to NASA's new astronaut selection round? They were trying to recruit women and minorities this time, he told her.

Kathy hadn't heard anything about that. She'd been living mostly in Canada, and news from the United States didn't travel northward very often or fast. Grant, still an aviation buff, had already applied to NASA. Throughout Kathy's break he pestered her to join him, pointing out that she had strong qualifications. "How many twenty-six-year-old female PhDs can there be in the world?" he asked her.

At first she thought it was an absurd idea. It was hard enough to study the ocean floor from just the surface of the earth. Putting hundreds of miles between her and the ground would only make things worse. So she brushed off Grant's pleas, returning to Nova Scotia with no plans to apply to some silly astronaut program.

A few weeks later, though, Kathy was thumbing through a science magazine when she saw an advertisement about the NASA selection process. The article explained that the astronauts selected in this round would fly on a brand-new type of vehicle known as the space shuttle. Their missions would be geared toward launching satellites and conducting science experiments.

And with science at the forefront of these missions, NASA was looking for more than just pilots. The agency needed people to fill the new role of "mission specialist." These astronauts would work mostly on science-related projects and wouldn't need any flying experience.

At that moment, Kathy realized that her voyages at sea might perfectly translate to voyages in orbit after all.

The First Women Who Tried

The Six and other women who applied to NASA's new program in the late 1970s were not the first women who tried to become astronauts. Fifteen years earlier a group of determined women pilots had fought for the opportunity—and almost gotten it.

NASA had kept women out of space since the agency had been established in 1958 by allowing only military-trained test pilots into the program, even though NASA was a civilian agency. The test pilots were usually healthy and fit. They were used to sitting inside cramped cabins and traveling breathtakingly fast. Because they were military, they knew how to take orders. And all of them were men.

There was no shortage of women pilots at the time. Many women had gained flying experience by the 1950s. A select group had even flown in the US during World War II, freeing up male pilots for overseas duty. But as the war ended, the military feared that men would come home from battle to find their piloting jobs taken by women. This also fit in with society's ideas in those days about what women should and shouldn't do. Many believed that unless women were needed for war work, having them take jobs outside of housework was a threat to traditional gender roles, even to national security. So the military barred women from flying its jets for the next three decades, meaning that the only avenue to becoming a test pilot was closed to women.

Yet even if this hadn't been the case, many women and people of color back then would have hit an educational barrier. Having flight experience was great, but at the same time NASA wanted college-educated engineers and scientists who could learn the ins and outs of the spacecraft they were piloting. Not many women and people of color had the degrees and experience that NASA desired. As challenging as it was for the Six to pursue their educational and career goals, women before them had been even more strongly discouraged from entering STEM fields. From 1950 to 1960, women made up only about 1 percent of all people employed as engineers, and between 9 and 11 percent of employed scientists.

A few people, though, wondered how women would do in space. One of them was Dr. William Randolph "Randy" Lovelace II, assigned by NASA to study how space travel affected the human body. At his New Mexico clinic Lovelace tested potential astronauts, whittling the pool down to the men who became the Mercury Seven. After a chance meeting in 1959 with Geraldyn "Jerrie" Cobb, a woman who'd gained thousands of hours of experience flying all over the world, Lovelace invited her to his clinic.

Research had started to suggest that women might be ideal candidates for spaceflight. They were typically smaller than men and weighed less, so they could more easily stuff themselves into tiny spacecraft, and it would require less rocket fuel to get them off the ground. They also performed better in isolation experiments. Lovelace was eager to put these possibilities to the test.

After a week of testing, Jerrie officially became the first woman to pass the same physical qualifications as the Mercury astronauts. "We are already in a position to say that certain qualities of the female space pilot are preferable to those of her male colleague," Lovelace said when he presented Jerrie's results to a conference on space medicine.

The announcement caused a sensation in the media. In an early hint of what the first women astronauts would go through, many articles focused on Jerrie's appearance or used terms such as "Space Gal."

Meanwhile, Lovelace tested another eighteen women pilots. Like Jerrie, they endured the same tests as the Mercury astronauts, swallowing a three-foot rubber hose to test the acidity of their stomach fluids, having ice-cold water squirted into their ears to test their ability to combat dizziness, and more.

Twelve of them passed Lovelace's tests. Three of the qualified women—Jerrie, Wally Funk, and Rhea Hurrle—took an additional challenge: floating in a dark, soundproof tank filled with water. It blocked their senses and created a true feeling of isolation. It was believed that people in the tank would start hallucinating after six hours. The women easily lasted for more than nine hours. Doctors eventually had to pull a completely calm Wally out of the water after ten hours and thirty-five minutes. The Mercury astronauts only had to last three hours in a dark, soundproof room.

All seemed to be going well for these women. NASA's administrator, James Webb, even appointed Jerrie as a consultant to the agency. Then, just as the women were about to experience simulated spaceflight at the US Naval School of Aviation Medicine in Florida, the tests were canceled. The navy had refused permission to use its equipment. The path to space was blocked again.

Jerrie and another of the women pilots, Janey Hart (whose husband was a US senator), fought to keep the program alive. They met with Vice President Lyndon B. Johnson, who was polite but not interested. As for NASA, it was focused on sending an astronaut to the moon, and many at the agency thought that training women would be a distraction from that goal.

Jerrie and Janey kept fighting. They managed to get a congressional subcommittee to schedule a three-day hearing on "qualifications for astronauts" in 1962. They hoped the hearing would convince the government and NASA of the merits of sending women into space.

On the first day, Jerrie told the committee, "Now we who aspire to be women astronauts ask for the opportunity to bring glory to our nation by an American woman becoming first in all the world to make a space flight." She pointed out that the Mercury astronauts had been required to have one thousand five hundred hours of flight time, and some of the women had more than ten thousand hours. Training women astronauts wouldn't take anything away from the space race or the goal of reaching the moon. Thirteen qualified women were ready. All they wanted was for testing to continue.

Everything changed on the second day of the hearing. A NASA director arrived, accompanied by astronauts Scott Carpenter and John Glenn. The men argued that hours spent flying airplanes did not compare with flying jets and test-piloting advanced aircraft. As for *why* women were not allowed to pilot jets—well, that was just a way of life.

"The men go off and fight the wars and fly the airplanes and come back and help design and build and test them," said Glenn, who'd become a hero just months before as the first American to orbit Earth. "The fact that women are not in this field is a fact of our social order." NASA might consider women astronauts someday, the men said. Just not now.

Even after these devastating statements, a few of the lawmakers made it clear that they believed NASA should strive to include women and study how to test them for future spaceflight. One directed NASA to create a program that would include women, in order to continue receiving congressional support. Again, though, that would happen in the future.

After that the lawmakers ended the hearing a day early. Jerrie and Janey were stunned. It was over.

Less than a year later, in June 1963, a Russian parachutist named Valentina Tereshkova climbed into a capsule atop a Soviet rocket after two years of training. She blasted off and orbited Earth forty-eight times. When Tereshkova returned, she'd spent more time in space than all the American astronauts combined. The Soviet Union, determined not to let the Americans beat them after hearing about Lovelace's tests, had sent the first woman into space.

Even though the US and the Soviet Union were locked in a battle of one-upmanship, sending women into space was a race that NASA didn't have much interest in winning. The United States, with traditional gender roles still influencing much of society, just didn't take the idea of women astronauts seriously, and so neither did NASA. As a result, the feet of women like Jerrie and Janey remained firmly planted on Earth as men soared above. The women who'd passed Lovelace's tests slowly faded into the background, never regaining the opportunity to train for space.

CHAPTER EIGHT

NASA Boldly Goes

★ ★ ★ ★ ★ ★

A woman punched a couple of buttons on the console in front of her. Switches lit up and blinked in response. She scribbled some notes in a notebook, then turned toward the camera.

"Hi, I'm Nichelle Nichols," she said, smiling. "But I still feel a little bit like Lieutenant Uhura on the starship *Enterprise*."

It was the spring of 1977. The hit TV show *Star Trek*—about a spaceship whose mission was "to boldly go" to new frontiers in space—had ended eight years earlier. But Nichelle was still famous for playing Uhura, an officer aboard television's most popular spacecraft. The show's many fans included young women and people of color around the world who had been thrilled to see a Black woman in that major role.

Today, though, Nichelle wasn't wearing the well-known short red dress that had been her Starfleet uniform on *Star Trek*. Instead she wore a different uniform—one that was also easy to recognize: NASA's deep blue astronaut jumpsuit. She was at the agency's Johnson Space Center in Houston that day to film a video that would advertise NASA's latest human spaceflight program.

Nichelle went on to describe the strange new vehicle that NASA was developing. It was called the space shuttle. This giant white-and-black space plane would be different from the earlier capsules that had been launched into space on rockets, then returned by parachuting into the oceans. The space shuttle would launch as a rocket, but it would land back on Earth like an airplane, which meant that it could make regular trips to and from space. One day, Nichelle said, it could even be used to build a space station in orbit around Earth.

Because the space shuttle was going to be so wildly different from earlier spacecraft, NASA needed a new crop of astronauts to travel inside it. "And this would require the services of people with a variety of skills and qualifications," Nichelle explained.

NASA still needed experienced pilots who could fly the space shuttle into orbit and land it on a runway back on Earth. But this time around the agency also wanted scientists, academics, doctors, and engineers, regardless of their time piloting a jet.

And, most of all, NASA wanted Nichelle Nichols to encourage women and people of color to apply.

No one of color had ever gone to space, and only one

woman had done so. That was Valentina Tereshkova, the Soviet cosmonaut in 1963, a year after NASA had blocked the group of qualified American women pilots from trying to become astronauts. Meanwhile, NASA had continued to send white men into space.

What had changed?

During the years in which NASA had kept sending the same kind of astronauts into space, the world below them had transformed. One big change had to do with attitudes toward women's roles and opportunities.

In 1963, that same year when Valentina Tereshkova flew to space, American writer Betty Friedan published *The Feminine Mystique*. The book examined the sexism that was present in all aspects of society and that pressured women to stay at home instead of striving for careers and goals of their own.

Sparks of a new social movement known as feminism, which calls for equality of the genders and for women to have the same rights and opportunities as men, had already been lit. *The Feminine Mystique* fanned those sparks into a flame. More than three million people read it. Soon a new wave of feminism spread as women sought reproductive rights, equal access to jobs, the ability to buy property and apply for credit cards without a man's permission, and more.

During those same years the United States also confronted racial inequality. Under leaders such as Dr. Martin Luther King Jr., A. Philip Randolph, and Ella Baker, the civil rights movement challenged long-standing racial prejudices and laws that had permitted discrimination by race. The fight for racial justice led to the passage of the Civil Rights Act of 1964, a milestone law that banned discrimination based on race, color, religion, sex, or national origin.

While these waves of change rolled through the rest of the country in the 1960s and 1970s, NASA was slow to keep up. The agency dodged question after question about when women and minority astronauts would fly.

But NASA couldn't hide from its failures forever. In 1972, Congress strengthened penalties for violating the Civil Rights Act. That same year NASA administrator James Fletcher finally began to hint that NASA was working on plans for people of color to fly aboard the new space shuttle.

Change wasn't happening fast enough, though, for a Black NASA employee named Ruth Bates Harris. She'd initially been hired to run NASA's Equal Employment Opportunity Office, but when she started, she was demoted to a lesser role. Still, Ruth repeatedly pressured NASA to open up jobs to more women and people of color. Finally, frustrated by her bosses' lack of urgency, she took matters into her own hands.

In the fall of 1973, Ruth and two coworkers wrote a

report that reviewed diversity and inclusion at NASA. No one had asked for such a report, but the three felt it was necessary. The report exposed NASA's efforts to recruit women and people of color as a "near-total failure."

Minorities made up little more than 5 percent of the entire NASA workforce. This percentage was "the lowest of all the agencies in the federal government." Women were slightly better represented, at 18 percent, but roughly 88 percent of those female employees were in the lowest-paying jobs.

And when it came to female representation in space, the report painted a grim picture: "There have been three females sent into space by NASA. Two are Arabella and Anita—both spiders. The other is Miss Baker—a monkey."

The writers cautioned that if NASA remained on its current path, minorities would make up only 9 percent of the agency by 2001. And they summed up the cost of doing nothing, saying, "An entire generation of people have been cheated from witnessing such [an] experience," of seeing a woman or a person of color go to space.

A month after Ruth and her coworkers submitted their report, NASA fired Ruth, calling her a "disruptive force" at the agency. But once the media found out about the firing, the backlash was swift. Newspaper headlines criticized the decision, lawmakers questioned it, and Senate hearings were scheduled.

Eventually NASA rehired Ruth in a different role, but there was no more sweeping that damaging report under the rug. The agency had to do something about its culture of admitting only white men as astronauts.

At the same time, NASA was in the middle of another great change. With the end of the Apollo program, the agency was turning away from deep-space exploration and toward a new model of space travel, focused on placing satellites in Earth orbit and doing research there. The space shuttle would be the primary ride for all astronauts, so crews would have four, five, or six people at a time. And that meant a wider variety of people with a wider set of responsibilities could be welcomed aboard.

During the 1970s many of NASA's astronauts were close to forty years old. Yet NASA didn't expect to launch the space shuttle for the first time until 1979. Agency officials realized that they'd need to bring in a new generation to crew the shuttle. And for the first time NASA would recruit two types of astronauts for those crews: pilots and mission specialists.

The mission specialist role was completely new. Mission specialists would launch satellites from the space shuttle, manage the shuttle's systems, and conduct experiments in space. Candidates did not have to be pilots, but they did have to have a bachelor's degree in a science- or engineering-related field, although an advanced degree was preferred. They still had to pass a physical exam, although the hearing and vision requirements were more relaxed than in earlier years, and they had to be between 5 feet and 6.33 feet tall.

In March 1976, the Johnson Space Center's astronaut selection board sat down to talk about how the agency would go about recruiting the new astronauts. The head of the board was a former air force pilot named George Abbey. During the Apollo program he had been the technical assistant to Chris Kraft, who directed the space center. Now, as director of flight operations, George would be tremendously important to the astronauts of the space shuttle program. Not only would he pick them but he would assign them to flights in the years ahead. And he was ready for his crews to look more like America—more diverse and more representative of the nation's people—than before.

He selected dozens of individuals at the center to help him. One was Joseph Atkinson, the first Black person to serve on an astronaut selection board. Another was Carolyn Huntoon, one of the most senior women at the space center. Chris Kraft had asked her if she wanted to apply to be an astronaut, but she'd turned him down. Instead she became the first woman on an astronaut selection board.

To tell as many people as possible about the astronaut selection, the board weighed the merits of advertising at universities, high schools, and civic clubs and organizations. They talked about sending out notices to newspapers and magazines. These were somewhat revolutionary recruiting tactics for NASA, which had typically relied on a "they'll come to us" approach.

For one member of the selection board, the changes were all too much. Deke Slayton, one of the original Mercury Seven astronauts, stood up during that first meeting, said, "I want no part of this," and walked out. It was an awkward moment, but not a very surprising one. "There was definitely a feeling that bringing women and minorities into the program was not necessarily a good thing," George said. "So it wasn't universally accepted."

The board didn't let Deke's outburst stop them. On July 8, 1976, NASA declared to the country: The agency is officially accepting astronaut applications. The deadline was June 30, 1977.

The board kept looking for ways to get the word out to as many potential applicants as possible, and that's where Nichelle Nichols came in. After filming the promotional video, she would travel the country, giving talks to students and encouraging a more diverse group of people to apply. "I am going to bring you so many qualified women and minority astronaut applicants for this position that if you don't choose one . . . everybody in the newspapers across the country will know about it," Nichelle recalled saying at the time.

In the video she filmed for NASA, Nichelle said, "The shuttle will be taking scientists and engineers, men and women of all races into space, just like the astronaut crew on the starship *Enterprise*. So that is why I'm speaking to the whole family of humankind—minorities and women alike. If you qualify and would like to be an astronaut, now is the time."

Carolyn Huntoon and many of the others on the board crisscrossed the country for months at a time too, giving talks. They wanted people of color and women to know that this time things would be different. But for some of the women Carolyn spoke to, the idea of a woman going to space sounded absurd.

"I can't imagine any woman who'd want to do that," one young woman told Carolyn.

"Well maybe you don't want to do it, and maybe I don't want to do it," Carolyn replied, "but there are young women in our country who want to fly in space. And they should be given that opportunity."

Among the women who wanted to fly in space were Shannon, Rhea, Anna, Sally, Judy, and Kathy. And once NASA's announcement reached them, they could at last apply for the chance.

Back then the application to become an astronaut was the same basic form used to apply for many jobs in the federal government. It asked for your name, work experience, education, medical history, and three references listing people who could vouch for you. To get one of these forms, you simply had to write to NASA's Astronaut Selection Office, and the necessary paperwork would be mailed back.

That's what Rhea did—in a way. When her colleague approached her in the hospital hallway and shared the news of NASA's astronaut selection, she vowed to learn more, but she didn't know how. About the only thing she did know was that the astronauts trained somewhere in Houston. So she sent a letter addressed to "NASA, Houston, Texas" asking for more information. The US Post Office somehow managed to get the letter to NASA, and Rhea received a reply telling her how to get the application. Soon the form was in her hands.

When Sally read about the astronaut selection in the Stanford paper, a spark lit inside her. She had the right qualifications. All she needed to do was fill out the form. She grabbed a sheet of paper with Stanford's Institute for Plasma Research letterhead and scribbled a quick request for information: "I am a PhD candidate in astrophysics at Stanford University, and am interested in the Space Shuttle Program. Please send me the forms necessary to apply as a 'mission specialist' candidate." She noticed she'd messed up one of her words when writing, so she scratched out the error. But rather than start over, she sent the letter as soon as possible. A form arrived roughly a week later.

Shannon didn't even need to ask for the form. After applying to many government jobs over the years, she had the correct form on hand. She filled it out the night she read about the selection in the magazine. Hers was one of the first applications to arrive at NASA.

Anna's might have been one of the last. With only weeks until the deadline, she and Bill sent for the application with little time to waste. Anna smiled as she wrote down "astronaut" in the box that asked what position she was applying for.

Kathy mailed her application in early 1977 and promptly forgot about it. With another expedition scheduled to the Atlantic Ocean to complete her PhD work, she dove into that.

In contrast, Judy's application process didn't end when she mailed the form. She'd made up her mind that this was what she wanted, and she threw herself into making it happen. She and Len Nahmi set out to make her look as good as possible to the astronaut selection board. She cut her hair because she believed it would look more professional. Then, equipped with some of Len's flight instruction manuals, she took flying lessons and picked up a pilot's certificate.

Judy also studied Apollo astronaut Michael Collins's book *Carrying the Fire,* mining his experiences for tips on becoming an astronaut. To get a better understanding of space history, she began visiting the National Air and Space Museum in Washington, DC. Once she even walked into the office of the museum's director, who happened to be Michael Collins himself.

"Hi, Mike, how are you?" she said. "My name's Judy Resnik, and I want to be an astronaut."

Rather than remove this stranger from his office, the man who had flown around the moon while the first astronauts had walked on it gave Judy some advice: "Learn everything you can about the Shuttle program."

It was good advice, but no one knew when or how NASA would make its choices. Judy could keep preparing, but she and everyone else who had applied simply had to wait.

CHAPTER NINE

Who Will Make It?

★ ★ ★ ★ ★ ★

The astronaut selection panel had up to forty slots to fill. By the deadline, 8,079 people—including 1,544 women—had applied. The panel had the pleasure of reviewing every single application.

Cutting everyone who didn't meet the published requirements brought the pool down to 5,680 candidates. The panel worked its way through many steps: grouping the candidates into their fields or professions, studying their applications, calling the people the applicants had listed as references, and asking for short interviews with applicants' families, friends, and coworkers. Eventually the reviewers settled on 208 candidates, including 21 women. The candidates would be invited to Houston in batches of twenty for a week of testing and interviews before the final choices were made. Now NASA needed to call everyone.

It was just another August day for Shannon at the Oklahoma Medical Research Foundation—until she received a phone call inviting her to Houston for an interview.

Rhea got her call at work too. She'd just started her

final year of residency. When she asked what would happen during the week in Houston, she learned that it would include briefings on the space shuttle, a physical exam, a psychological evaluation, and an hour-and-a-half-long interview.

"Will there be any other women?" Rhea asked, her mind racing.

"Yes," the caller said. "Eight of you."

In California, Anna and Bill were at home, going over wedding plans, when the phone rang. Anna answered and listened, wide-eyed. She then covered the phone with her hand and said to Bill, "It's NASA. They want me to come in for an interview." But there was a catch. She needed to be in Houston during the week when she and Bill had planned to get married.

There was another catch. NASA was calling just for Anna, not Bill.

"Say yes, and we'll figure it out," said Bill.

They got to work and arranged to get married sooner. After a whirlwind four days of planning and an overnight "honeymoon" to San Francisco, Anna came home to San Pedro, worked two full shifts in the ER, and got on a plane to Houston.

After Sally received her call, she made one of her own. "I'm going to Houston for an interview," Sally told her childhood friend Sue Okie over the phone in September 1977.

The news came as a total shock to Sue, who had never heard Sally mention wanting to be an astronaut. Sally told her friend she had known it was what she wanted to do with her life ever since she'd seen the announcement of a new round of astronaut selections in the Stanford newspaper.

By the time Judy got her call, she was living in California too. She had taken a job at the Xerox Corporation. She had also continued what she saw as her second job: prepping to become an astronaut. Every morning she jogged along the beach across the highway from her apartment to get into top shape.

She'd told her father about applying, and his response had been, "Good, Judy. So you'll become an astronaut."

"Oh, Daddy. There will be thousands of others applying."

"So what? Of course you're going to be accepted." When the call came, those words were a step closer to becoming true.

When Kathy's phone rang in October 1977, it wasn't NASA on the line. It was a professor at Columbia University asking if she was going to accept a position working on his project studying the marine geology of the deep sea. It would let her fulfill one of her dreams: diving to the ocean's depths in the *Alvin* submersible.

"Oh, yes," came Kathy's reply. "Well probably."

Kathy explained that she'd applied to NASA's astronaut program and was waiting to hear back. Coincidentally, the professor had applied to NASA's astronaut program himself, back in the 1960s. He'd even become a finalist before getting cut. Knowing how the process worked, he told Kathy to let him know when she found out where she stood.

So, unlike the others, Kathy was the one who called NASA. She discovered that she was scheduled for an interview the following month and just hadn't gotten the message yet.

Stunned, Kathy called the professor back. She then called her mother.

"What exactly does this mean?" her mom asked.

"It means that when I finish my degree I'm either going two hundred miles up or six thousand feet down."

NASA's interview process began in August 1977 and would last for months. Every other week a new group of twenty showed up at the Johnson Space Center (JSC), fresh-faced and hopeful, ready to tackle the activities that NASA's officials had cooked up.

Each interview week began with an orientation meeting on the first evening. This was the candidates' first chance to size up the competition. Many of the military men knew each other already. So did some of the academics. But most of the women felt like fish out of water, even though many of them shared the same credentials: MDs and PhDs. Kathy would later say, "I felt very much out of place."

On that first night George Abbey asked everyone to do a simple homework assignment. He wanted each of them to write an essay on why they wanted to be astronauts.

Late into the evening the women wrestled with how to express their dreams of launching off the planet. They had no idea what the selection panel was looking for. So they simply tried to be honest.

"I've been fascinated with space ever since those early telecasts, but never really thought it would be possible for me to become an astronaut—my chances of getting certification as a test pilot appeared pretty slim then," Sally wrote on her sheet of paper.

Rhea wrote, "I also think it is time that women be allowed into the program—not only because they have a great deal to offer—but because it is time that we knew how they will fare in space—and what special problems they will face there."

Before heading off to bed, Anna wrote, "I realize that there will be certain significant sacrifices which I must make in both my personal and professional lives in order to become a mission specialist astronaut but those are sacrifices which I thoughtfully and willingly will make if given the opportunity to fulfill a lifetime dream."

The day after their arrivals, the trials began.

Candidates had to endure many physical tests. They ran on treadmills with breathing tubes over their mouths while physicians monitored their blood pressure. They sat on a rotating chair designed to test their balance and sensitivity to motion sickness. Each candidate had twenty-four types of physical exams and lab tests, as well as a checkup from a NASA flight surgeon. But the agency was just as interested in psychological fitness. NASA wanted people who could react well under pressure and easily get along with others, so each candidate had two psychiatric evaluations as well.

Everything felt like a test. When NASA officials encouraged the candidates to explore the center and talk to current JSC employees, to get a better sense of what working in Houston would be like, some of the women wondered if it was a trick. Did NASA really want them to walk around? And were agency officials watching and listening in on their conversations with other employees?

Despite their misgivings, the women did explore the space center. One day during some downtime, Sally discovered the racquetball court in the gym. Two male candidates were swatting balls against the wall, so she asked if they were interested in a game. They said yes, not knowing of Sally's tennis history. "She proceeded to destroy both of us," one of the men said. Then she thanked them for the game and left to go running.

As Anna walked around the campus, she started to get a feeling that this place might become home, and she wanted her husband to come visit too. Eventually Bill would come back for his own interview in November. He and Judy were in the same group. After Judy and Anna realized they lived close to each other in California, they became friends and stayed in touch.

The real test for each candidate was an hour-and-a-half-long interview with the selection board. NASA deliberately told them nothing about what they would be asked. The selection panel wanted to get to know them as they really were.

The interview was basically one big question: "Start in high school, tell us what you did there, and bring us up to now," George Abbey would say at the start. Sally described her tennis background and her graduate work with free-electron lasers. Judy talked about her work with the National Institutes of Health and learning more about the human eye. Rhea and Anna both detailed their medical work. Kathy discussed her deep-sea missions, and Shannon talked about her chemistry experience.

Shannon, Judy, and Rhea also had piloting experience, so they spoke of their time in the air. Many of the women mentioned that they'd been fascinated by the early space-flight missions.

As the candidates spoke, members of the board asked questions. Most of those questions were about the candidates' professional lives, but eventually the questions got personal. Candidates were asked about times when they overcame struggles and what they liked to do in their spare time. Then came the family questions.

One panelist asked Rhea, "What if, on the plane going back to Memphis this weekend, you meet the man of your dreams and he asks you to leave your medical career, give up the chance to become an astronaut, and go away with him?"

The question annoyed Rhea, who didn't think it was appropriate. She was the first woman to be interviewed, and she thought there were still a few kinks to work out when it came to questioning women. She answered truthfully: he wouldn't be the man of her dreams if he asked her to do that.

Anna also tried to be as honest as possible, including in her choice of outfit. She wore a long green one-piece pantsuit with thick-wedged heels—typical fashions of the 1970s. That was her style. She figured NASA knew everything about her already anyway, so she might as well be true to herself. When the question of children came up, she was honest about that, too, saying, "I want to have children, so if that's a factor in your selection, I definitely do want to have children." She hoped it wasn't a deal-breaker.

As for Shannon, she already had children—three of them. She waited for someone to ask her, "How can you possibly do this job with three kids?" Years of battling with former employers over the issue of being a working woman *and* a mother had primed her to answer this question.

It was never asked. Instead someone said, "This job

requires a lot of travel. Do you have any problems traveling for work?" Considering that she was applying to travel into space, it was a funny question. But Shannon knew that being an astronaut meant more than traveling off-world. It required flying around the country to train for missions and meet with scientists, engineers, and the contractors who were building the space shuttle and the equipment it would carry into space.

"Absolutely not," she said. "I travel now." She explained that she and her husband, Michael, had a simple arrangement. When she traveled for work, he took care of the kids. When he traveled, she did. There was no reason their responsibility-sharing couldn't continue.

Some candidates agonized over basic questions, such as if they wanted a Coke. Some tried attempts at humor, as Sally did when one interviewer asked, "Have you ever had amnesia?"

"I don't know. I can't remember," she joked.

There were no right or wrong answers. The panel was looking for certain traits. The selection board wanted team players. Mission members would need to cooperate and rely on each other. The panel also wanted people who could be flexible, with interests in more than one field. Advanced degrees were impressive, but the board looked for hobbies or side projects—an interest in flying, maybe, or playing classical piano, or tennis. Space shuttle crews needed to be the kind of people who could learn multiple things. During their missions they'd need to understand a variety of disciplines, from engineering and rocketry to astronomy and earth science.

But most of all the board tried to find out if the candidates really wanted the job they'd applied for. "We wanted to make sure that they understood what the job was because a lot of people had an impression of what astronauts do—and it's quite different than what the astronaut job really is," said George.

The shuttle's first flight was scheduled for 1979. Its early missions would be flown by astronauts who were already in the space program. This new class of astronauts wouldn't sit in the shuttle's seats for years. Most of their work would be on the ground. They would run experiments, do simulations (gamelike activities that closely imitate the process of operating aircraft and spacecraft), learn software and new technologies, and make public appearances for NASA.

The selection board wanted people who understood that going to space was a small part of the job. And a few of the finalists wound up deciding that the job wasn't for them.

But not these six women. Like all the other candidates, they flew home after seven days at the Johnson Space Center. And each of them yearned for the day when their telephone would ring and a NASA official would be on the other end.

But once again, just as after they'd mailed in their applications, all they could do was wait.

CHAPTER TEN
"This Is Your Friendly Local Astronaut"

★ ★ ★ ★ ★ ★

The interviews ended in November. The anxious candidates didn't know it, but by late December, NASA was getting close to sharing their decisions.

The panel had agreed on forty candidates—twenty pilots and twenty mission specialists. With so many astronauts still waiting to fly, though, NASA's administrator questioned the need for twenty new pilots, leading George Abbey and his team to shave off five of the twenty.

Meanwhile, the candidates who had been to Houston waited desperately for their calls as December came and went with no word.

The women had returned to their normal lives. For Shannon that meant working in the lab and caring for her family. Judy chugged along at her new job at Xerox. Anna and Rhea put in long shifts at their hospitals. Sally and Kathy each worked toward the last year of their PhD programs. It was life as usual . . . but with NASA on their minds. Especially for one of them, who had already seen the space shuttle.

In late October, Sally had visited Edwards Air Force Base in California's Mojave Desert to see the shuttle in action. NASA was conducting landing tests with a space shuttle named *Enterprise* that had been built for test flights in Earth's atmosphere. As Sally and some of the other astronaut candidates watched, the giant vehicle traveled into the sky on the back of a large airplane. Then the airplane separated from the shuttle and flew away, leaving *Enterprise* to return to Earth on its own, with two astronauts flying it. But when the spacecraft touched down on the concrete, its massive tires bounced, causing the whole thing to wobble. A wing tipped. *Enterprise* bounced a few more times before coming to a final stop.

The test landing didn't make Sally feel particularly secure about becoming an astronaut.

"Up until this morning I wasn't afraid at all," she wrote in a letter to Molly, who was living in New York. "It never entered my mind that there were actual risks involved. But seeing that landing this morning, knowing that they couldn't pull up for another try—that scared me."

When Rhea's phone finally rang in January 1978, it wasn't NASA. It was Jules Bergman, a reporter who had covered the space program and the Apollo flights. He wanted to talk to some of the women who'd interviewed for the job. Rhea agreed to meet him at the hospital on January 15.

During the interview Jules asked basic questions about Rhea's background and why she wanted to be an astronaut. Then he dropped a bomb.

"Would you believe you've been picked as one of the first woman astronauts?"

Rhea thought it was a joke or a what-if question, but he assured her he had heard it "through very good sources."

Rhea fought back her excitement. She'd look ridiculous if his information turned out not to be true. Smiling, she told him she'd still be surprised if she got the call.

"Well, I can guarantee you: you have been selected," Jules said.

"Well, I'm very excited then," Rhea said, laughing.

"They'll be calling you—early in the morning."

"Well, that's what I want to do with my life, and it just . . . It'd be very thrilling to hear that," Rhea said.

Across the country in California, Judy called Anna the same day as Rhea's interview. Judy felt that something was about to happen. She'd been getting calls from reporters, and she wanted to know if Anna was hearing anything too. Sure enough, Anna was getting the same weird requests. The two wondered, *Does this mean we've been picked?* "We kind of had an idea that something was up, but you didn't want to get your hopes up too much," Anna said.

When the women went to bed that night, some were

unable to shut their eyes, wondering what the next day might bring.

On Monday morning, January 16, 1978, George Abbey picked up his office phone before sunrise in Houston. He had thirty-five calls to make that day, and no time to waste. NASA was going to send out a press release that afternoon, announcing the newest astronauts, and the news was bound to make a splash. Among the thirty-five people selected, three were African American and one was Asian American, NASA's first astronauts of color.

Also within the group: America's first six women astronauts.

The first number George dialed was a Canadian one.

The ringing telephone jolted Kathy Sullivan and her roommates awake in their apartment in Halifax, Nova Scotia. Her roommate picked up the phone, listened, and turned to Kathy in awe. "It's somebody from NASA."

She passed the phone to Kathy, who heard George's voice on the other end.

"Are you still interested in coming to work for NASA?" George mumbled, with the same calm tone as someone asking for a small favor. This question would be George's opening line throughout the day.

"Yes!" she cried, completely taken aback.

George worked his was westward across the country. Soon he was dialing Tennessee. Rhea was on her way to work, still buzzing from her interview the day before. As soon as she arrived, the hospital's operator informed her that she had a call from NASA. The women at the hospital's reception desk stared at her eagerly while she took it. "Are you still interested in coming to work for NASA?" George asked.

"Yes, sir!" Rhea managed to blurt out, feeling as if she were about to dive off a cliff.

A few minutes later Shannon spoke to George from the Oklahoma Medical Research Foundation. He asked his question, and Shannon sang out, "Of course!" Her lifelong dream was coming true. Later she gleefully broke the news to her husband, who was thrilled. The couple then tried to explain Shannon's new job to their children, who didn't quite understand what it all meant. The best explanation Michael could come up with was, "Your mommy might be like Mr. Spock in *Star Trek*."

Sally's phone rang at around five or six a.m., while she was still asleep. Groggily she picked it up to hear George on the other end, asking if she was "still interested." Thinking it might all be a dream, she replied, "Yes, sir!"

Right after she hung up, she rang her friend Sue Okie. "Hello, this is your friendly local astronaut," Sally said. From then on that would be how Sally greeted Sue on the phone.

Judy had just walked out the door to go to Xerox when

she heard her phone ringing in her apartment. Wondering if it might be the Call, she sprinted back inside. She accepted the offer, thrilled that her hard work had paid off (and relieved that she'd turned around that morning).

Just a few miles from Judy, the phone rang at Anna and Bill's home, but the circumstances there were quite different from the other candidates' homes. An NBC camera crew had asked to film the couple while they received word from NASA. The crew was standing with them in their kitchen when Bill answered the beige telephone. He turned to Anna with a smile, and said, "It's for you."

"Are you still interested in coming to work for NASA?" George asked. She replied, "Oh, you know I am! I don't know what to say except thanks so much. We've been thinking about it and thinking about it. I hope I can do a good job for you all."

Anna handed the phone back to Bill, who then became the only candidate to get a rejection from George—the others who didn't make the cut were called by other panel members. But Bill handled it with grace and hugged Anna when he hung up. The couple had prepared for every possible outcome. They had felt that if only one of them got picked, it would probably be Anna, who had more graduate experience in physical sciences.

While the women excitedly called family and friends with the news, the wider world soon found out about their historic selection, and the questions began. At NASA's press conference a reporter asked why it had taken NASA so long to choose women to fly to space. "I think that in the last few years in the United States that—because of the women's movement frankly—that women are much more qualified," said Chris Kraft, the head of the Johnson Space Center. He added: "And in this particular case, we found a very large number of women that were as well qualified as the men."

By that afternoon the entire country knew about the Six, and each of their phones began shrieking nonstop as reporters tried to reach them for interviews. It was just a taste of the media storm that they would face at every step of their journey to space.

The thirty-five new astronauts reported to the Johnson Space Center at the end of January for an orientation session. It included a press day when the astronauts would officially be revealed. NASA employees and members of the media gathered inside an auditorium. As camera bulbs flashed and reporters scribbled in their notebooks, Chris Kraft welcomed everyone to the event. Then he began reading out the names, in alphabetical order, of what was now officially known as NASA Astronaut Group 8. One by one the new astronauts walked out to take a seat on the stage.

The first was Guion "Guy" Bluford. He was one of

three Black men NASA had selected. The other two were Frederick Gregory and Ronald McNair. Guy and Fred had been air force pilots. Ron had graduated from MIT with a PhD in physics. Also in the group was Ellison "El" Onizuka, a test pilot and engineer. He was from Hawaii and was the first Asian American astronaut.

After Chris had read a few names, he got to Anna Fisher. She was first of the six women selected to take the stage. Although she showed no emotion, trying to hide her nervousness, she broke out into a smile when one of the men next to her leaned in to make a joke. Soon Shannon was called. Then the alphabet placed Judy and Sally next to each other. Rhea and Kathy came near the end of the roll call.

With all the seats filled, the media—and the country— now had its first look at the most diverse class of astronauts yet. The group was still dominated by twenty-five white men, but it was closer than NASA had ever come to picking astronauts who reflected the true makeup of America.

When it was time for individual interviews, perhaps for the first time, the white men found themselves ignored. The media wanted to talk to the historymakers. Eventually the lopsided press attention led the astronauts to refer to themselves as "ten interesting people and twenty-five standard white guys."

Before the women confronted the ravenous press corps, they met with Carolyn Huntoon, from the selection board.

She knew what the Six were about to face, so she gathered them in a hallway for a pep talk. The media would want to know as much as possible, and what the Six said would have a lasting effect on how people viewed women astronauts.

How each woman answered their questions would spill over to the rest of the group. That meant that if one woman revealed private information, the press would try to get that same level of detail from the others. Carolyn told them to expect questions about their relationships, their makeup and exercise habits, and more. Now was the time, she said, for the Six to stand united. They could decide together what they were comfortable talking about—and what was off-limits.

In those brief moments ahead of their first interviews, the women decided to be open, to a degree. They were taxpayer-funded employees, after all. Facing the public was part of the job. But the media didn't need to know every detail. The women resolved to keep their private lives private.

Then it was off to the wolves. The Six broke apart for their separate interviews.

Journalists asked whether the women felt different from their male counterparts. "We all look at ourselves as just one of the guys, one of the astronauts, not as men or women," Judy told a reporter at the *Houston Chronicle*.

They asked who wanted to be the first American woman in space. "I just want to be a person going into space," said Anna. "I don't really think it is important who the first woman is."

After the first round of interviews, the women found themselves in the hallway again, heads spinning. One of the Six saw an opportunity and shouted, "Potty break!" They swiftly gathered in the nearby ladies' restroom. Most of the reporters and NASA employees were men, so that bathroom was the first chance the women had to be alone. They talked about the reporters who had interviewed them.

"Who did you have?"

"What did he want?"

"What did you tell him?"

After pooling information and practicing some answers, they scattered to meet their next round of questions. Those bathroom meetings became a routine that day. Not only did they help the women cope with the press but they were also the first chance for the Six to form a united front.

After the media whirlwind, orientation ended with a dinner hosted by the man who was about to become their boss, George Abbey. The new astronauts mingled and introduced themselves to the people who'd someday become their crewmates, friends—and, in some cases, spouses.

A tall redhead named Steve Hawley introduced himself to Sally and the other doctoral students. Originally from

Kansas, Steve had been in Chile studying astronomy before his selection. He felt comfortable around the other graduate students and academics and took particular notice of Sally.

Whatever barrier had existed between the military and civilian recruits began to break down. Rhea introduced herself to two navy pilots, Mike Coats and Robert "Hoot" Gibson. Judy met John Fabian, an air force engineer, and Frederick "Rick" Hauck, a navy pilot and engineer who'd graduated from MIT.

Not all of the men were excited about their new colleagues, though. Mike Mullane, an engineer and weapons system operator for the air force, didn't say it that night, but he viewed the women and the other civilians with suspicion. To him these baby-faced graduate students didn't have the right life experience to fly to space—not the experience that military astronauts had gained during the Vietnam War. And he was not prepared for working with women.

He wasn't the only man there who felt that way. Still, the night was one of celebration. Everyone had just met the people they'd be flying with. This new chapter of their lives, one of space exploration, was beginning.

But not quite yet.

The group was told to report for duty first thing July 10, a little more than half a year away.

Mobbed by the Media

Even before the women were selected, the media focused on them. When the candidates came to Houston for their NASA interviews, the women were more in demand than the men for photos and quotes. As soon as Anna, Rhea, and Shannon arrived at the Johnson Space Center in the first batch of candidates, a mob of journalists shoved cameras and lights into their faces. Reporters asked why they wanted to be astronauts. Everyone wanted to know more about the first women that NASA was interviewing to go to space.

Some of the men felt jealous of all the attention. The women, meanwhile, gave quick answers and moved on. They didn't know it, but that was just a fraction of what was to come. Once their selection was announced, the media demanded more.

So many media people thronged Rhea's hospital that her bosses had to hold a press conference. Stanford University did the same for Sally. There media people surrounded her. Some of the questions they shouted were ridiculous. "Aren't you afraid of being in orbit with all those men?" TV crews also showed up at Sally's house, wanting to film her daily run.

To have each other as support, Judy and Anna agreed to a joint interview for the *Los Angeles Times.* "I think that when there are as many women astronauts as men it won't be a novelty any longer and the interest will naturally fall off," Judy said, then added, "NASA should have had women involved with the space program many years ago."

Reporters also desperately wanted to know if Bill was bitter that Anna had been picked and not him. "It's fantastic that Anna was chosen, and I feel no resentment," Bill later told a reporter.

It was both thrilling and overwhelming for the Six, who had no training in dealing with the media. "One day I was a doctor working in medical training," Anna said. "The next day I was an astronaut. But nothing had happened in that twenty-four-hour period. I didn't know any more than I knew the day before. . . . So that was a baptism by fire."

Over the next few days the women started to understand just how many eyes were focused on them. Talk show producers offered to fly them to New York City for whirlwind visits and interviews. Newspapers printed close-ups of their faces on front pages. The major networks all asked to visit the women at their homes and at work, to get a peek inside their daily lives.

A CBS News crew profiled Rhea and Shannon in their hometowns. The crew wanted to know how Shannon would juggle her responsibilities as a mother and an astronaut. "Well, I've always worked and I've always put in a lot of hours," Shannon replied. "My oldest daughter, her great discovery when she went to first grade, she came home one day and said, 'Guess what, Mommy? Did you know that some mothers stay home all day and never go to work?'"

Shannon found the attention fun, but it soon started to feel a bit invasive. The CBS crew had filmed her at home while she made dinner. After that she decided she didn't want the press coming to the house or interacting with the children. "I mean, this was *my* job; it wasn't a family job," she said.

As much as they tried, the women could only do so much to control how the press presented them—or to push back against the sexism that tainted many headlines and articles, a sign of what they would continue to face. Newspaper and magazine writers described them with minimizing, cutesy terms such as "Glamornauts" and "eye-popping space gals." Less silly, but still not respectful, were "girls" and "ladies in space." In another kind of unequal treatment, the women's marital status, age, height, and weight were often included in their descriptions, while the male astronauts were rarely described in these ways.

Only a few reports conveyed the historical significance of the new astronauts. ASTRONAUTS HURDLE SEX, RACE BARRIERS, one headline read. Another was MEN ASTRONAUTS TAKE BACKSEAT IN NEWEST CREW LINEUP.

But the media frenzy over the nation's first women astronauts was only beginning. And on the day when one of them would be named as the first American woman to go to space, she'd face even more overwhelming attention.

CHAPTER ELEVEN

An Astronaut's Job

★ ★ ★ ★ ★ ★

In the summer of 1978, each of the Six moved to a new home to start her new NASA life.

Judy was the first to get a taste of Houston's steamy summer weather. She quit her California job, packed her things, and came to Houston a couple of months before she was officially needed.

Kathy and Sally finished their PhD work before leaving for their new lives. Kathy then traded in the cold of Nova Scotia for the Texas heat, while Sally road-tripped to Houston through the Southwest, with her physicist boyfriend, Bill. Thanks to help from Carolyn Huntoon, NASA gave Bill the status of a spouse, even though he and Sally were not married. Living together without being married was still something of a taboo in the 1970s, although it was becoming more common.

For Shannon and Anna, moving involved other people. Each of their husbands had to find work in Houston. Bill Fisher also signed up for graduate courses in engineering and trained for his pilot's license, hoping to improve his chances of being chosen in the next astronaut selection.

No matter what path they had taken to get there, bright and early on Monday, July 10, the Six made their way to the Johnson Space Center, southeast of central Houston. In a large conference room they and their twenty-nine male classmates anxiously awaited their first assignments. They weren't the only astronauts in the room, though. Every Monday morning there was an all-astronauts meeting, so the conference room also held twenty-seven astronauts who had been chosen in earlier years. Some had flown on Apollo and Skylab missions. Others had not yet made it to space.

The two groups—the oldies and the newbies—sized each other up. The first thing people noticed were the wrinkles or the lack of them. Most of the current astronauts were in their forties, pushing fifty. Many of the new ones were in their twenties and thirties. Tension filled the air as each group felt intimidated by the other. Everyone wondered how they should interact with the new faces in front of them.

Another divide cut between the military and civilian astronauts. Those with military backgrounds shared similar behaviors, expectations, and humor. For them, learning to fly a new vehicle, even one as advanced as the space shuttle, would be somewhat familiar. The women and the male researchers came from backgrounds such as universities, hospitals, and businesses. For them the world of NASA was truly uncharted territory.

But beyond these differences each astronaut knew that everyone else was competition. There was only so much room on each space shuttle flight. Every person in that room was someone else who could fill an empty seat they wanted to be in.

The Six had shared a bond since their bathroom retreats on that first press day, but one thought tugged at them all.

Only one of them would be the first woman to fly.

At the meeting the thirty-five new astronauts—technically called ASCANs, for "astronaut candidates"—learned what lay ahead. Two long years of training were required for them to prove they had what it took to fly to space.

The ASCANs would learn the ins and outs of the space shuttle's systems, so that each could step in during a flight to fix any part that was failing. They'd tour NASA's various centers to better understand what every part of the agency did. They'd learn an array of scientific and engineering disciplines, to better handle the satellites and experiments they'd take to space. And they'd fly in pairs in NASA's fleet of T-38 jets, to get a feel for operating a high-powered vehicle in the air.

NASA didn't waste any time getting started. After the meeting the newbies scattered to their first science lessons.

Before training got into full swing, though, they had to come up with a nickname—something catchier than "NASA Astronaut Group 8" or "ASCANs." The nickname tradition had begun with the Mercury Seven, the first astronauts. The newest astronauts decided to call themselves the Thirty-Five New Guys, the TFNGs for short. The women appreciated being seen as part of the larger group. "We didn't want to become 'the girl astronauts,' distinct and separate from the guys," said Kathy.

Now that women were part of the astronaut corps, though, NASA did have to make some necessary changes. Women hadn't been much considered when many of the facilities at the space center had been built. The biggest change made before the Six had arrived was a new women's locker room attached to the gym, with women-specific features such as hair dryers.

Still, the Six were keen to blend in as much as possible, down to the outfits they wore. On one of their first days at work, Anna and Sally sneaked off to a nearby store to shop for single-color polo T-shirts and khaki pants. This bland outfit was the unofficial uniform of the male astronauts and engineers. Going forward, it would be theirs as well.

But where the Six really had to prove themselves was in their training.

Because the astronauts would spend a lot of training time in the T-38 jets, NASA wanted to ensure that those who didn't have flying experience in jets could bail out of the cockpit in an emergency. That meant parachute survival training for the women and other new recruits.

In late July, NASA flew them to Homestead Air Force Base in Florida. There they would learn to survive a bailout over open water. For three days the astronauts suited up in jumpsuits and strode through one-hundred-degree heat to nearby Biscayne Bay. There, waiting for them, were their parachuting instructors—and the media.

Why the media? NASA's job was first and foremost to send people and spacecraft into orbit, but promoting itself was also vitally important. That's because NASA's budget came from lawmakers, and to keep receiving this funding, NASA was constantly driven to showcase all the ways in which it was using taxpayer money well. The agency didn't pass up good photo opportunities and the publicity they brought. Especially not an event as juicy as water survival training.

Reporters and television crews were on hand, and predictably, everyone wanted a piece of the Six. One reporter called out for Sally to give him a "happy look," to which she simply replied, "No!" Another tried to get Rhea's attention by yelling, "Hey, Miss." Rhea shot back, "It's Doctor." The male astronauts were again ignored, which prompted one to remark to a reporter, "We're mere commoners."

After giving a few quotes, the women focused on the

task. Buckled into their harnesses, they were dragged by ropes behind speeding motorboats through the shark-filled waters. The goal was to keep their faces above the waves. This could save their lives if they ever parachuted into choppy seas, with high winds pulling their parachutes to and fro.

The Six also had to swim beneath floating parachutes, practicing how to survive if the canopy came down around them. Once they'd emerged from under the chute, they'd inflate their life vests and wait for a helicopter to pluck them from the water.

Finally, they sprinted off the deck of a boat with parachutes attached to their harnesses, letting the wind sweep them four hundred feet into the air at the end of a rope. Then, when given a signal, they disconnected from the boat and drifted down to the water, as if bailing out from a jet. Once they hit the bay, they had to inflate a life raft and crawl on top.

For many of the women it was the most exciting and exhausting day of their professional lives. The barges filled with gawking reporters didn't help. "We're under enough stress doing things that we've never done before, especially the nonmilitary folks," Rhea recalled later. "Keep the press away from us." At one point during the training, Sally thought, *What am I doing here? I'm supposed to be a smart person.* But everyone came out of it smiling.

Ejecting from a jet over water was one thing. Coming down over land was another. A few weeks later the Six found themselves at Vance Air Force Base in Enid, Oklahoma, not far from where Shannon had grown up. There, on a painfully hot day, they suited up for round two.

They sprinted again with bulky parachutes hooked to their backs. This time, though, they ran across land as a pickup truck pulled them by a rope. Eventually they soared into the air, then released themselves and floated down. They had to position their legs just right in order to land safely.

Anna was one of the smallest in the class. Almost immediately the wind whipped her into the air, while the taller members of the group were dragged by the truck until a strong gust got them airborne. Unlike after water training, the Six left land survival training battered and bruised. But they held their tongues. As far as NASA knew, they'd loved every minute of it.

With survival training complete, it was finally time for the good stuff: climbing into NASA's sleek T-38s at the Ellington Field airport. These jets could fly faster than the speed of sound and reach altitudes ten thousand feet higher than a standard commercial airplane. Their curved glass cockpits were just large enough for a pilot and a back-seat rider to fit inside.

NASA wanted all the mission specialists who weren't

jet pilots to spend at least fifteen hours each month in a T-38. The women were officially designated as back-seat riders, forbidden from taking off and landing the jets themselves. But they'd still help to handle the aircraft in the air, working together with their pilots, communicating through headsets, navigating through cloudy skies, and getting slammed into their seats.

When it was time to fly, the women crammed themselves into the tiny back seats, strapped oxygen masks to their faces, and braced themselves as the T-38s practically leapt off the runway. Their first flights got the women used to accelerating through the air and hearing the sounds of the cockpit over their headsets. Later they got their hands on the controls, temporarily taking the role of pilot.

Sensitive to even the slightest movements, the T-38s required the lightest touch on the stick to bank or climb. Each new flight challenged the Six to become ace jet pilots. During one flight the women would find themselves being tested on their knowledge of instruments in the cockpit. On another they'd have to develop a cross-country flight plan, mapping out where to stop for fuel. But perhaps the most exhilarating flights were the ones that turned the world upside down.

The TFNGs performed aerial maneuvers forty thousand feet above the vast Gulf of Mexico. They would fly in tight formations, their T-38s soaring through the air together like a flock of birds, wingtips just feet apart. Then they'd execute backward loops, barrel rolls, and other mid-air acrobatics.

If the pilots turned the aircraft just right, they could give their back-seat riders a heaping dose of extra g-forces, increasing the pressure of gravity and making it feel as if an invisible weight was slamming them into their seats. This was the same feeling they'd experience if they made it into the space shuttle cockpit and climbed into the sky.

It all could be stomach-lurching stuff. But if any of the Six did get truly airsick, they kept it to themselves. Just as with their survival training, they didn't want anyone to think they couldn't hack it. "You realized that there was this added burden of wanting to make sure we succeeded so that we didn't at all affect the women who would come after us," Anna said.

Shannon, who had thousands of hours of flight time by this point, took to the T-38 with ease. However, NASA wouldn't let her get fully trained and certified to pilot the T-38. The agency required most of the TFNG mission specialists to stay in the back seats. Shannon pointed out that another of the TFNGs, pilot Frederick Gregory, had experience comparable to hers but still got to fly in the front of the T-38.

"But, Shannon, he flew in Vietnam and got shot at," one NASA official told her.

"Well, if I go out over the Gulf and get somebody to shoot some bullets at me, *then* can I get checked out?" she replied. Unfortunately, her request didn't work.

Being limited to the back seat meant that the Six were at the mercy of the pilots' schedule to get their flight hours. They had to find a pilot who happened to be going somewhere and hope their back seat was unoccupied. The Six quickly learned that not all pilots were the same. Some hogged the controls and didn't speak during the entire flight. Others earned praise as "50 percenters," pilots who'd let the women have the stick for half the flight. Still others were thrill-seekers who liked to play dangerous games in the sky.

Eventually the Six found the pilots they loved flying with the most. Rhea gravitated to Hoot Gibson, to whom she'd introduced herself at the astronaut presentation. For her it was about being comfortable, and Hoot, a TOP-GUN pilot, knew a great deal about air traffic coming into and out of major airports. He'd prep her on what to say over the radio.

Judy, Sally, and Anna often found themselves in the back seats of jets piloted by Rick Hauck, John Fabian, Dan Brandenstein, and Jon McBride. Shannon often flew with John Creighton, who also happened to be her office mate. Technically the women and other mission specialists weren't allowed to fly below five thousand feet. But a few pilots were known to look the other way, giving the women the opportunity to take off and land the planes.

Both Sally and Judy became highly skilled pilots. The men were amazed at how quickly they adapted to the controls, as if they'd been flying for years. Hooked on this new pilot life, Sally even began taking private lessons on the side, eventually working to get her license. So did Anna, who would later complete her first solo cross-country flight in a Cessna 150.

And being a good flier went a long way at NASA. "The truth is that most of the skills you need to be a good shuttle crew member, you learn in the jets," said Steve Hawley. "It's things like crew coordination. It's flight planning; it's talking on the radio; it's hand-eye coordination. If you're actually flying the jet, it's actually having to deal with real emergencies." The better the TFNGs performed in the T-38, the better they looked as potential crew members in space.

Most of the TFNGs' time, though, was spent in the classroom. For those with advanced degrees, that felt a bit like home. But whatever their academic background, they all had to start thinking like engineers.

They took classes on every part of the space shuttle. Other classes covered the sciences that would be involved in experiments done on the space shuttle or on the payloads, which were the cargo, such as satellites, that the shuttles would carry into orbit. Because much of this activity would involve studying Earth from space, the TFNGs studied the planet's geography and oceanography, which Kathy had mastered. Classes on astronomy were a piece of cake for Sally. Doctors Rhea and Anna breezed through the lessons in human anatomy and medicine that prepared crews for medical emergencies.

When they weren't in the classroom or the T-38 cockpit, the TFNGs spent the rest of their time traveling throughout the United States. NASA had nearly two dozen centers spread throughout the country. This was a way for the agency to have employees in many states—and win support from those states' lawmakers.

Each center had its own specialty. The TFNGs toured the Marshall Space Flight Center in Huntsville, Alabama, which oversaw the production of the space shuttle's massive external fuel tank and its rocket boosters. They flew to the Kennedy Space Center in Cape Canaveral, Florida, home of the launchpads where the space shuttles would take flight. (The Cape would become the astronauts' second home.)

They also visited the Jet Propulsion Laboratory in Pasadena, California. Engineers there designed and crafted the robotic explorers—uncrewed satellites, probes, and landers—that studied the solar system. During that visit a few astronauts learned that not everyone at NASA supported the space shuttle program. "I'll just never forget the director getting up and telling us that, 'We really [don't] need you guys,'" Hoot Gibson recalled.

Trips around the country were equal parts learning opportunities and public relations. The astronauts would also be shipped off to the headquarters of NASA's fleet of contractors, the companies that made its equipment. Not only would the astronauts learn a little more about the equipment that would help the space shuttle get off the ground but their smiling faces would boost company morale.

The Six also became intimately familiar with another plane, a massive one that could give its passengers a brief taste of the weightlessness of space. When the pilot flew this craft in a series of moves at high altitude, the passengers experienced brief periods of extra g-forces and free fall (zero or ultra-low gravity), one after the other. During free fall the astronauts could float around the padded cabin for thirty seconds at a time.

The shifts between weightiness and weightlessness often meant that people's stomach contents floated around the cabin too. The plane was nicknamed the Vomit Comet, after all. But the Six trained to keep lunch down by enduring up to fifty peaks and valleys in the aircraft.

There was never any complaining, no matter how tough or unpleasant the training became. The Six were determined to project confidence in everything they did, even when the pressures seemed overwhelming.

As Anna had said, the Six understood that as the first women astronauts, all eyes were upon them. They were watched more closely than their male colleagues. They also realized that if one of them visibly messed up, critics would pounce. Any failure could be called evidence that women weren't fit for space. So when Rhea struggled with scuba training, she cried at home because she feared it would end her astronaut career, but she showed up the next day determined to press forward.

No one could see a hint of fear or weakness on their faces. But underlying everything they did was a silent awareness of the enormous risk they were preparing themselves for. On one particularly serious training day, the TFNGs listened to a recording from January 1967.

They heard the voices of astronauts Gus Grissom, Ed White, and Roger B. Chaffee, the three crew members of the Apollo 1 mission. The three had been in the tiny capsule on top of their rocket for a launch rehearsal.

"Hey! We've got a fire in the cockpit," Ed yelled over the speakers.

Roger's voice sounded next, "We have a bad fire!"

The TFNGs listened to the final moments of the three, and after it was over, everyone in the room stayed silent.

It was a solemn reminder of what they risked in this job. And why their training was a matter of life and death.

CHAPTER TWELVE
Meet the Space Shuttle

The space shuttle was going to change everything.

That was NASA's dream when it cooked up the program in the early 1970s. This new 122-foot-long black-and-white space plane was meant to turn spaceflight from something dangerous and expensive into something cheap, routine, and safe.

NASA imagined the space shuttle as America's most sophisticated truck. It was expected to make routine trips to and from low Earth orbit, just as a semitruck hauls cargo across the country. And just like a truck, the space shuttle would be open for business. It could carry all sorts of payloads to orbit for customers.

Although rockets without people on board had been putting satellites into space just fine for more than a decade, NASA hailed the shuttle as the perfect platform not just for launching commercial satellites but for carrying out science experiments in ultra-low gravity, also known as microgravity. In addition it would be a great place to study Earth from above. NASA also sold the space shuttle as the ideal ride for the Department of Defense's supersecret spy satellites. And when NASA was ready to build a space station, the space shuttle would carry sections of it into orbit.

The shuttle's main feature was its payload bay, a cavernous cargo hold that took up most of the vehicle's body. Once the space plane was free of Earth, two massive doors would open, exposing the bay's contents to the vacuum of space in order to release the heat from the shuttle's electronic systems. If astronauts had to do something in the bay, they'd wear space suits. Or they could use a new tool being developed for the shuttle, a robotic arm that would be operated from inside the crew cabin. The arm, attached inside the bay, could latch on to things and move them through space.

Like past rockets, the space shuttle would take off vertically, driven by three main engines at its base. But with wings on its sides, a vertical tail at its base, and a flight deck overlooking a nose cone, it looked much more like an airplane than a rocket.

Also unlike past rockets, the shuttle couldn't contain the amount of liquid propellant needed to get the giant craft into space. The highly flammable propellant—made up of liquid hydrogen (fuel) and liquid oxygen (oxidizer)—would be held in separate compartments in a massive orange bullet-shaped external tank under the shuttle's belly. The tank would weigh more than 1.6 million pounds when filled with propellant. During launch the fuel and oxidizer would funnel out of the tank and into the shuttle's main engines, where the mixture would combust. When the propellant was used up, the tank would fall to Earth.

Even with this huge external tank, the shuttle's main engines couldn't get the spacecraft all the way to orbit. The pull of Earth's gravity was too great, and the space shuttle was too heavy. So white rockets more than one hundred fifty feet tall sat on either side of the external fuel tank. They ran on solid propellant, a mixture of hot-burning materials, to give the space shuttle the extra boost it needed to reach orbit.

In fact the boosters would be the largest solid rockets ever flown and the first to send humans to orbit. There had been concern about solid rockets being safe enough to carry such precious cargo, because unlike rockets that run on liquid propellant, a solid rocket cannot be turned off. Once it starts burning, it must burn through all its propellant. If something went wrong during a flight, the solid rocket boosters would keep thrusting the craft forward, whether the people on board wanted them to or not.

If that didn't give the astronauts and mission managers enough to think about, making the solid rocket boosters was complicated as well. A company called Thiokol was the main contractor. It built the rockets at a factory in middle-of-nowhere Utah. But Thiokol couldn't ship the rockets in one piece to the launch site in Florida. They were too big for any land vehicle or plane to carry. And Utah didn't have waterways for barges. So the company manufactured the boosters in segments, each as big as a railcar could hold, and shipped those by train to Cape Canaveral.

Engineers in Florida then stacked the segments on top of each other, with seams between them. To keep the flames of the booster rockets from escaping through these seams, two thin rubber rings known as O-rings were placed inside each joint. These seals were the first line of defense to prevent the scorching gases produced inside the rockets from escaping.

A lot of moving parts had to work together just right to get the space shuttle and its crew to orbit. But one major feature of the shuttle was a huge advantage for NASA. Earlier astronauts had come back from space in tiny capsules with parachutes that splashed down in the ocean. The space shuttle, on the other hand, would be piloted home to land on a runway, so that it could be used again. The solid rocket boosters would also parachute down and could be reused.

Reusability was seen as a key to opening spaceflight up to the masses. It was also expected to save NASA enormous amounts of money. An early study from NASA and the Defense Department predicted that the space shuttle could eventually make thirty to seventy flights a year, which would lower the cost of getting cargo into space.

First, though, the newfangled spacecraft had to fly.

• • •

When the TFNGs joined NASA in 1978, they and every-one else expected the space shuttle to fly by the end of the following year. George Abbey had already chosen two astronauts of long standing as the crew of the first shuttle mission. They would be the commander and pilot of STS-1—the first flight of the Space Transportation System, the shuttle's technical name. They'd also be the world's bravest guinea pigs, flying on the new *Columbia,* the first shuttle to be completed after the test vehicle *Enterprise.*

But the astronauts would soon learn that a NASA time-line can always change.

The space shuttle's road to the launchpad developed unexpected bumps. One was that the new main engines NASA had developed for the shuttle kept blowing up during testing. Each explosion brought a new set of prob-lems to figure out.

Another bump had to do with the thirty thousand insulating tiles that covered the outside of the shuttle. Made of silica fiber, the tiles were essential protection for the vehicle's return to Earth. They kept the shuttle from burning up as the air around it heated to nearly three thou-sand degrees Fahrenheit.

The tiles had to fit together on the outside of the shuttle like pieces of a puzzle. Each one had to be glued on indi-vidually. It could take up to forty hours for each tile. And some of the tiles just wouldn't stick. That's why the first space shuttle arrived at its launch site half naked.

A 747 airplane carried *Columbia* from California, where it was built, to Florida for its first flight. When it arrived, the shuttle was missing about seventy-eight hundred of its tiles. Workers continued to install them, but many that had already been glued on were breaking and had to be replaced.

NASA finally found a way to strengthen the tiles so they would stick for good, but the engine and tile problems, among other final issues, delayed *Columbia*'s first launch by two years. This frustrated NASA and government officials—and astronauts. But every part of the system had to be flight ready and safe, because the Space Shuttle lacked a proper escape. Once the solid rocket boosters ignited, the spacecraft was committed to launching until the rockets burned out after two minutes. Only after the boosters separated from the vehicle could the crew try to do something if a major system malfunctioned.

If one of the liquid-propellant engines malfunctioned on the way up, the shuttle might still reach orbit. Or it could skip orbit and try to land across the Atlantic Ocean, in Europe or Africa. The most dangerous option was the dreaded "return to launch site" scenario, in which the shuttle would try to flip over in the air and land back where it had started. All these possibilities depended on the space shuttle holding together. If it broke apart during flight, the astronauts were helpless to change their fate. But NASA needed them to be ready for any emergency. And that meant practice. Lots of practice.

To train crews to fly on the space shuttle, NASA created two types of simulators. These full-sized mock-ups of the vehicle's cockpit had all the seats, screens, and switches the astronauts would use during flight. One simulator stood still. The other moved and shook like a ride at a theme park, giving the sensation of bursting into the sky.

The TFNGs watched as the astronauts who had already been picked as crew members used the simulators. They saw the crew run through their preflight checklists and try to overcome possible malfunctions. Notorious NASA trainers known as Simulation Supervisors would pose outrageous worst-case scenarios to challenge the crew. Sometimes the astronauts juggled the catastrophes to land safely back on Earth. Other times their efforts failed, and the crew were told that their vehicle was breaking into thousands of pieces, which would have been fatal to the entire crew if it had been real life and not a simulation. If that happened, it was time to start again.

While the TFNGs yearned to sit in the simulators, each of them had their own engineering assignments to keep them busy. Almost immediately the Six began to wonder what these assignments meant for their futures. In their minds some jobs were good and others bad.

Sally snagged a juicy gig. Her first assignment was to work with the space shuttle's fancy new Remote Manipulator System (RMS), or as it would become known, the robotic arm. This snakelike mechanical device was manufactured in Canada. It functioned a bit like a human arm, but with more freedom of movement.

The robotic arm was so light that it couldn't carry its own weight on Earth, but in the microgravity environment of space, it could lift and move objects weighing thousands of pounds. Astronauts on board the shuttle would need to use the arm to pluck payloads out of the cargo bay and place them in orbit. The arm could also be used to grab on to satellites that were in space and put them into the bay.

The arm wasn't easy to control, though. Astronauts in the shuttle's cockpit had to manipulate its controls while looking at video screens that showed its position. Translating what they saw on screen into small muscle movements required impressive hand-eye coordination. Sally the tennis pro seemed to excel at it. She'd come home from work and tell Bill that she thought she was pretty good at this robotic arm thing—better than many of her colleagues.

Judy began by studying all sorts of software, but eventually she found herself assigned to the robotic arm too. She, too, took to it with ease, and it became her specialty. Soon Judy was flying back and forth between Canada and Houston, helping create procedures and develop software for operating the arm. Many in the astronaut corps soon realized that being good with the arm was a way to stand out.

Anna's first assignment was also a big one: testing space suits. NASA was developing new suits for the space shuttle, and George Abbey wanted to see if the agency's engineers could develop extra-small suits to fit the more diverse body types now in the astronaut corps. This was necessary because suits during the Apollo era had been custom-made for individual astronauts. Moving forward, though, the space shuttle suits would work a bit like a Mr. Potato Head. Astronauts would choose the torso section that best fit them, then attach the various-sized arms and legs to complete the suit.

The problem was, NASA hadn't finished these new suit parts yet. So for her testing Anna had to wear an old Apollo suit worn by Pete Conrad, the shortest of the astronauts who had walked on the moon. Pete might have been small, but the suit still swallowed Anna, making the simplest tasks a challenge.

Space suits are really the world's smallest spaceships, in the shape of a human body. They must contain enough atmospheric pressure to keep the person inside alive, but moving the arms and legs of an inflated suit is difficult. Having the right-sized suit is key to getting anything done. "For the smaller women if you can get a good suit fit, they can do just as well," said Anna. "But if you don't have a good suit fit, you're lost."

A couple of days a week she'd get into Pete's space suit, like a small child playing dress-up in her big brother's clothes. A team of divers, photographers, surgeons, and more would help her into a giant pool in the Weightless Environment Training Facility (WETF), the closest thing on Earth to simulating the weightlessness of space. She'd spy people taking her picture and waving at her, making her feel like a lab rat. But this was just how NASA operated. An astronaut had better get used to people watching their every move.

In the end NASA decided not to develop the extra-small space suit. "We're not discriminating. We're trying to be economical," a space suit technician told a reporter. "You've got to draw the line somewhere." Yet the decision meant that many of the women, when they did go to space, would be unable to conduct space walks—the most thrilling part of a mission, when suited astronauts performed tasks floating in space.

Meanwhile, Shannon's assignment took her to SAIL— the Shuttle Avionics Integration Laboratory. This facility housed a working space shuttle cockpit, where astronauts could test out software. Shannon loved it, but others feared assignments that took them away from the main Astronaut Office. They worried that being away from the rest of the team—and George Abbey—would hurt their chances of getting picked for a flight.

Kathy feared this when she was assigned early on to test

NASA's WB-57F aircraft, a vehicle designed to fly at extremely high altitudes. On paper it was an awesome gig. Kathy would get certified by the US Air Force to fly while wearing a pressure suit in the thin atmosphere—the first woman to earn such a certification. But her assignment took her to an air base more than five miles away from the Johnson Space Center campus. Kathy grew concerned that she might be forgotten, but she decided to make the most of it. The pressure suit she'd wear was the same one the crews on the first four shuttle flights would wear. Perhaps, she thought, she could turn this experience into wearing an actual space suit one day.

Rhea wasn't thrilled with her assignment, to help craft the food systems. "I ended up with the cooks," she'd say later. She'd hoped for something more technical as a way to learn more engineering. After a friend said they thought the assignment was sexist—reflecting the old idea that working with food was a woman's job—Rhea questioned it even more. But she tried to be optimistic, telling herself she'd been picked because of her background in nutrition.

Besides, no one argued with George's decisions. So Rhea threw herself into the assignment and was soon flying on the Vomit Comet with the new food packets the NASA engineers had designed. Her task was to test what happened when they were squeezed in microgravity. Sometimes these tests happened while astronauts were being tested for motion sickness in a spinning chair. When the smell of fresh spaghetti and Parmesan cheese wafted over to the spinners, an upchuck was likely to follow.

The truth was that the assignments were supposed to be confusing at first. George deliberately put people in jobs where they would be uncomfortable. "We put scientists in operational jobs, military test pilots in science, and so on," he said. "They had to be generalists, and they had to be able to cope with assignments that went beyond their experience."

The Six toiled away for months. With a year left to go, their training seemed never-ending. But one day in August 1979, Chris Kraft showed up at the Astronaut Office with an announcement. The TFNGs were no longer astronaut *candidates*. Their two-year training period had been cut short. There was simply too much to do to prepare for the first flight of the space shuttle, and the TFNGs had progressed faster than expected.

In honor of their accomplishment, each of the new astronauts was awarded a small silver pin. But they all knew they'd *really* become astronauts when they flew—and they wouldn't fly until the shuttle did.

On December 29, 1980, that day came a lot closer.

Carried on a platform the size of a baseball field, the completed space shuttle *Columbia* inched toward one of the launchpads at the Kennedy Space Center. In just a few months it would take off from that spot.

George had made sure that most of the astronauts had some kind of job associated with the upcoming flight. With their medical training, Rhea and Anna were assigned to search-and-rescue. If the shuttle had some kind of abort or crash during the flight, they'd be on hand to help save the crew. On launch day they'd work with elite para-jumpers who would ride in helicopters and parachute down to the crew if they crashed back on Earth. The doctors prayed their expertise wouldn't be needed.

Rhea had been named head of the doctors, so she had her choice of where to be at the launch. She chose Cape Canaveral, of course, to see the space shuttle take off. She and the para-jumpers would be ready if the shuttle had to double back after takeoff and perform the "return to launch site" that everyone feared.

Meanwhile, Anna would be at NASA's landing strip in the bleached landscape of White Sands, New Mexico. The shuttle could land there if it had to abort the mission after one orbit around Earth. Also stationed in White Sands would be Shannon, who'd pulled chase duty. If the shuttle did come in for a landing at White Sands, she and another TFNG would hop into a T-38 and chase the vehicle through the skies, gathering as many images and as much information about the shuttle as possible, to report back to NASA.

The days ticked by. Many tests were performed as the shuttle sat on the launchpad. Finally, in April 1981, it was ready to fly. For their assignments Kathy and Judy had been offered to the major television networks as experts. They repeatedly studied their notes so that they'd quickly recall key space shuttle facts when asked by eager reporters.

Kathy had been assigned to ABC. Apollo 17 moonwalker Gene Cernan was already booked as the TV expert, so Kathy provided commentary on ABC Radio. Not only did she not have to dress up for radio, but the ABC radio booth was three miles from the launchpad, with a clear view. Kathy would have a front-row seat to a history-making flight—and still be able to wear a comfortable outfit.

But at one point Kathy overheard Gene say something wrong about the shuttle's computer systems. She asked a nearby producer if it mattered. "Next thing I knew," Kathy recalled later, "I was up on the TV set with Frank Reynolds—me happily dressed in radio casual. I was now on national television and facing the delicate challenge of contradicting the famous veteran astronaut sitting across from me on the news desk."

Just a few yards away, Judy was on camera sporting a bright pink blouse at the NBC News setup. In the days before the launch, during a segment on women astronauts, Judy had answered NBC anchor Tom Brokaw's questions about training. Then questions about dating had come up—questions that the men were never asked.

"What happens when you meet a man who's not in the

space program and doesn't know who you are, and you say, 'I'm an astronaut'?" Tom queried. "Does he say, 'Ah, you're too cute to be an astronaut. Come on, little lady, you can't be an astronaut'?"

With a wide smile, Judy gave a diplomatic reply. "I just tell them I'm an engineer."

But he continued to ask questions that were not just uncomfortably personal but downright sexist. "What about the whole business about social relationships? . . . Are some men threatened by the fact that you're an astronaut?"

"I don't know," said Judy. "If they are, they're probably not my friends."

A moment later he asked, "Do you think the time will come when there will be romance in outer space?"

"Oh gee, I couldn't tell you that," said Judy.

It was a long couple of days.

Longer still when *Columbia*'s first launch attempt on April 10 had to be scrubbed due to software issues. But two days later, with crowds of spaceflight enthusiasts packed onto the beaches under Cape Canaveral's crystal-blue skies, the flight controller led space shuttle *Columbia* through the final countdown:

"Seven. Six. Five. Four. We have gone for main engine start. We have main engine start. We have liftoff of America's first space shuttle and the shuttle has cleared the tower!"

Sally watched in awe from the sky, looking out the

back-seat window of a T-38 miles from the launchpad. Hers was perhaps the best assignment of all. A different form of chase duty, she'd been assigned to follow the launch in the air. She watched as *Columbia* climbed, powered by its main engines and solid rocket boosters, looking like a small, upside-down candle against a backdrop of vibrant blue. The space plane got smaller and smaller, until it disappeared from view.

High up in the sky, the two solid rocket boosters broke away and fell to Earth after two minutes of burning. Over the next six and a half minutes, *Columbia*'s main engines drove it to the speed needed to reach orbit—nearly 17,500 miles per hour.

Eight and a half minutes after launch, *Columbia* reached its orbit, putting it into a continuous loop around Earth. A crucial moment came right after that: main engine cut-off, or MECO. The flames shooting from *Columbia*'s main engines disappeared while the shuttle coasted through the vacuum of space. Seconds later the external tank broke away. Smaller engines embedded in the space shuttle fired for a few seconds of extra oomph.

Two days later *Columbia* touched down in California. And seven months after that it flew another two-day mission. The first reuse of a spacecraft that had carried a crew to orbit proved that the shuttle could do what had been claimed.

The era of the space shuttle had arrived.

CHAPTER THIRTEEN

Working with Men

★ ★ ★ ★ ★ ★

New eras were beginning for the astronauts on the ground, too. The Thirty-Five New Guys were no longer the newest guys. Before *Columbia*'s first launch, nineteen new astronaut candidates had joined the corps. This diverse group included two women, Mary Cleave and Bonnie Dunbar. It also included Anna's husband, Bill. Anna no longer had to hold in her excitement about work when she came home. She and Bill could talk about NASA, and Anna could give Bill tips on ASCAN training.

The Fishers were the first astronaut spouses, but not the last.

Hoot Gibson had been married when he'd begun his astronaut training, but he and his wife had divorced soon after. After some time sharing a T-38 on frequent flights, Rhea let Hoot know that she had feelings for him, and they began dating. A month after *Columbia*'s first mission, the two TFNGs got married in her hometown of Murfreesboro, Tennessee. They were the first astronauts to marry while in the corps.

While good relationships like theirs formed, it wasn't all smooth sailing between the men and women, especially at first. When the Six first arrived at NASA, they felt some initial unease. Many of them were used to working with mostly men, but here they were especially outnumbered. After all, just three years earlier women had made up only 17 percent of NASA's workforce, and mostly as technicians or in clerical jobs.

Many of the men in the astronaut program came from a hyper-masculine military background. They cracked sexist jokes and seldom considered whether these might offend their new female colleagues.

At times the Six found themselves struggling to be taken seriously by major figures in spaceflight history. Alan Bean, an Apollo astronaut who had walked on the moon in 1969, told *Texas Monthly* that at first many older astronauts felt that the incoming women were doing men's jobs. "I know I felt that," Alan said. "Astronauts, to me, were men; they had to think about computers and flying—male things."

Once, Kathy and her astronaut partner landed a T-38 in California for a day to train for chasing the space shuttle on an upcoming flight. They spotted Chuck Yeager, the famed test pilot who'd been the first to break the speed of sound. When Kathy's partner introduced her to Chuck and told him she was flying chase, the old test pilot scrunched his mouth and said, "Riding, maybe. Ain't flying."

NASA's male engineers also had to get used to working with women as their peers. The engineers had become accustomed to the male astronauts talking to them as equals. But when one of the Six spoke up, a few of the male engineers became flustered. They weren't used to women questioning their decisions.

The sometimes-chilly reception didn't come from just men. The Six also ran into friction from other women—the wives of their coworkers. During the first few weeks of training, a few of the pilots weren't too keen on flying with the Six. They blamed their wives, who weren't comfortable with women spending hours a few feet from their husbands. One astronaut said to Carolyn Huntoon, "I think it's great we're having women astronauts. It's my wife who doesn't think it's so good."

"That's not our problem," Carolyn said, pushing back. "That's not the women's problem. That's your problem."

Sexism had been expected, at least by Carolyn. She and other NASA officials did not kid themselves that accepting women as astronauts was universally popular. But NASA was pressing forward anyway. "It's not like we were taking a vote," said Carolyn. The time had come for change in the roles of women, both at NASA and in society. Those who weren't ready for it could not stop it from happening.

As one of the few women in a senior position at the Johnson Space Center, Carolyn was ready to offer help and advice to the Six on how to navigate JSC as a woman. And if there was ever an issue that the Six needed to address as a unit, Carolyn would hold informal meetings with them to hash things out.

One meeting was about the huge amount of attention the Six were receiving. The public affairs office at NASA would often accept appearance requests on their behalf and ask them to talk to various groups or do interviews. It was starting to weigh heavily. Each appearance took a lot of work and effort. Sometimes the women missed several days of work and training time.

Carolyn understood their frustration, but she advised them to lower the volume. "By complaining about it all the time, they were really offending the guys who weren't being asked at all," Carolyn would later recall.

The Six felt that they could rely on one another when needed, and they were ready to pounce if they saw sexism in action. One such incident took place when a male astronaut tried to keep Kathy from being treated as an equal. During the third flight of the space shuttle, she was assigned to work at the Cape, where NASA had leased a three-bedroom condo at the Kennedy Space Center for the astronauts to use. But when Kathy asked one of her teammates for the key to the condo, he grew flustered. He told her that he was worried about how it would look if two guys stayed in the same house as a woman. "What will people say?"

Annoyed though she was, Kathy let him say his piece before responding as politely as she could. "I think how we handle it is entirely in our hands," she said. "I think we just need to saddle up and go do it."

He said he'd think about it. But when Kathy let the other women know what their colleague had said, they all let him have it. "What are you going to tell your wife when I'm assigned to a crew with you?" they asked. They reminded him that neither the media nor his wife would get a say in his flight assignments. It took him a day to finally give up and hand over the key.

But although the Six were trusted coworkers who had each other's backs when necessary, they didn't see a lot of each other. Shannon, in particular, was too busy to socialize, with three young kids at home. "When I wasn't working, I was home taking care of my kids and doing all the things that you do with kids," said Shannon. She added, "Life was extremely full."

And some of the Six grew closer than others. Rhea and Anna were both doctors married to other astronauts. Their shared experiences gave them a stronger bond than with the other four. Sally and Judy had similar senses of humor and were both fiercely driven. They were natural friends.

Another factor was that the Six spent more time with their male colleagues than with each other during training. Because the Six were all back-seaters in the T-38s, all their flying time was spent with male pilots. During trips that lasted hours, the women and men chatted over their headsets. Over time the Six found themselves closer friends with their male colleagues than with each other. And that meant putting up with the men's teasing and pranks.

And the TFNGs didn't discriminate in their teasing. Everyone was a target, men and woman alike. If you made a mistake on the job, you were likely in for ribbing. On the eve of the third shuttle mission, Kathy had to go over the thousands of switches in the vehicle's cockpit. After hours of struggling to keep her eyes open, Kathy hit the wrong button when trying to radio Launch Control. Suddenly all the buttons in the shuttle's cockpit lit up. Alarms blared. She had accidentally switched the shuttle's main computers into emergency backup mode.

The mistake threw Launch Control into a panic. Over the radio the team spit out rapid-fire suggestions about possible malfunctions. Mortified, Kathy confessed. Later the shuttle launched just fine and on time. But Kathy knew she was in for it.

When she walked into the party after launch, she was braced for ridicule. The launch director handed her a gift, a gray metal box with two large buttons on it. One was labeled THIS ONE, the other NOT THIS ONE.

Not to be outdone, Kathy solemnly announced that she'd already punished the culprit responsible for the accident. She held up her hand. A large bandage wrapped around her thumb made it look as if she'd tried to cut it off. Everyone cracked up.

Just as they'd hoped, over time the Six were closer to becoming "one of the guys." And if the guys ever did treat them like anything but fellow astronauts, they'd shut it down. Hard. Sally, especially, made it crystal clear she wouldn't tolerate being treated differently. Once, Hoot watched in amusement as a male astronaut held the door open for her. Smiling, she shoved him through the door and opened it for herself.

Sally wouldn't put up with 1950s-era behavior, and neither would Judy. A male colleague once introduced her in front of an audience as "one of our six lady astronauts." Judy walked onstage and promptly joked to him, "I'm no lady."

After a few hiccups in the beginning, the women came to feel that NASA was embracing them. They were part of the team. Even the skeptical male astronauts came around. Alan Bean, who'd doubted the wisdom of having women become astronauts, changed his opinion, possibly because he'd spent time mentoring Rhea. He eventually said, "The job of astronaut is just as female as it is male."

Ultimately the TFNGs became a family. It was impossible not to, given how much time they spent together. They took turns throwing parties at their homes each week, went on camping trips, and even planned out-of-this-world excursions, such as seeing a total solar eclipse from a T-38. Judy in particular was fast becoming friends with her TFNG coworkers. She earned a reputation for being able to hang out with men on their own terms. She and John Fabian grew close as they traveled to and from Canada to work on the robotic arm. "Judy was my best friend in the Astronaut Office," John later said. "I thought the world of her."

Romances bloomed too, and not just Rhea and Hoot's. Steve Hawley had been interested in Sally from the beginning. As he got to know her, he felt that they had a lot in common. Both were scientists focused on space. Both were avid fans of the LA Dodgers baseball team. And they always seemed to find themselves in the same place at the same time.

But when Sally had arrived at NASA, she'd still been living with Bill Colson. Months later Steve heard that Sally's relationship was ending. "I wasn't particularly fitting in," Bill confessed. Sally had wanted him to try becoming an astronaut, and he'd even taken flying lessons with Bill Fisher. But he realized his heart just wasn't in it. He and Sally broke up, although they kept in touch as friends. After that, Sally and Steve eventually became a couple.

By the time the next group of candidates had entered the astronaut program and the space shuttle was flying, the Six and their fellow TFNGs were having the time of their lives, forging bonds they knew would last for decades. And all of them yearned for the day when they'd get the call from George Abbey, telling them they'd been assigned to a flight.

But for the Six there was an extra question: *Which of us will be first?*

CHAPTER FOURTEEN

Becoming "the One"

★ ★ ★ ★ ★ ★

One of our standard adages in the office was 'There's no such thing as a bad spaceflight,'" said Kathy. "But flying sooner is better than later. A longer flight's better than a shorter flight. High inclination is better than low inclination"—referring to the route the space shuttle took around Earth—"and space walks are wonderful."

But astronauts weren't picky. "When in doubt, refer to rule number one: there's no such thing as a bad spaceflight," recalled Kathy.

By spring 1982 three space shuttle missions had flown. Crews were already assigned for the next three. It was time to choose the first TFNGs to fly as part of the crews for the three after those: STS-7, STS-8, and STS-9. Each mission had its own unique requirements. George Abbey's choices would be based on those requirements—and something more.

America was about to see its first Black astronaut fly. And its first woman. One of the Six was about to become the One.

BECOMING "THE ONE" • 133

Sure, technically she wouldn't be the first woman to fly in space—that had been the Soviet cosmonaut Valentina Tereshkova. But one of the Six would be the first American woman. That would hold tremendous weight. Her name would be added to the list of US spaceflight pioneers. She'd be a pathbreaker mentioned in history books for centuries—and an instant hero to millions of young women. Becoming the One would bring fame, contracts, speaking fees, and a larger-than-life identity. The other women would do groundbreaking work too, but their names wouldn't echo as loudly or for as long.

Though Anna had once told a reporter that it wasn't important who went first, the silent competition among the women had begun almost as soon as the astronaut class had been formed. It played out first in newspapers and magazines and on television broadcasts. The media seemed to slot the Six into female "types"—and to favor those who fit a more traditional, feminine image of womanhood.

Anna, for instance, was something of a media darling. With her award-winning smile she had a classic charm that the press loved. What's more, she eagerly gave interviews when asked. Her face appeared in many magazines, and she often appeared on TV to talk about the merits of the space shuttle program.

Anna's willingness to perform for the media wasn't a calculated move to put her at the front of the pack. She wanted to do whatever it took to keep the shuttle program afloat. "I just felt like, if there's anything I can do to get good publicity and to get this space shuttle off the ground so that I have the career I want to have, I'll do it," she said.

But over time it seemed as if Anna had become the face of the astronaut corps. And when Bill was selected as an astronaut in 1980, the press's fascination with Anna and her husband only grew. They became America's first astronaut couple, catnip for the ravenous media. A MARRIAGE THAT WAS MADE FOR THE HEAVENS, the *New York Times* declared.

The conventionally attractive blond surgeon Rhea wasn't far out of the press's sight either. Pictures of her in the Gulf of Mexico during water survival training, or floating weightless in the Vomit Comet with a grin spread across her face, popped up in newspapers and magazines. And when she and Hoot married, the press was delighted. Now the country had two astronaut couples—an idea that had seemed foreign just a few years earlier.

The other members of the Six saw it all playing out before their eyes. And they knew where they stood. "If you were going to line the six of us up, put our six photos up, and pick cover girl shots, I'm not a cover girl type," said Kathy. "I've been on covers, but I'm not an archetypal cover girl look or face; neither is Shannon." Sure enough, the media tended to emphasize Kathy's larger size compared to the other women astronauts. And Shannon, the tallest and already a mom of three when she came to NASA, was quickly cast by the media as the mother figure of the bunch, somewhat less exciting than the singles and newlyweds.

While Sally and Judy could have been considered "cover girl types," they had little interest in playing to the press. Sally tried to keep the media at a distance because she was shy, never one to seek the limelight. She'd gotten an early taste of the press when she'd first started at NASA, and she didn't like the idiotic questions asked by the mostly male reporters. She preferred talking to Lynn Sherr, a female reporter at ABC who focused more on the astronauts' missions and training.

Judy felt that her life was none of the press's business. She didn't like media attention on her relationships, especially her divorce. And she didn't want to give the public a guided tour of her complicated upbringing. So she rarely gave interviews, and when she did, her answers were short. America heard very little about Sally and Judy in the shuttle program's first years.

NASA wasn't openly grading anyone on their star quality, but everyone knew that the One would face a flood of speaking requests and TV appearances. The astronauts' public relations value would probably be part of the decision. Weighing her chances at the time, Kathy recalled, "I've got to bet there's some big factor that, all other things being equal, they will pick a cute one who gets on lots of covers. This is all guys making this choice. Somehow that's in there. So that probably means Anna, Judy, Rhea, and Sally have a qualitatively better chance of getting the nod first than me or Shannon."

Shannon also felt the politics at play underlying the decision. For her, being the One wasn't really the goal. She just wanted to work and do a good job. Most of all, like any other astronaut in the corps, her overarching ambition was to fly. And according to Kathy's rule, flying sooner is always better than later. "Being first was one thing, but you want to fly as soon as you can," Shannon said. "Waiting is hard."

The astronaut corps was also looking closely at the Six, placing imaginary bets on which woman would be picked first. Everyone kept a watchful eye on the assignments the women received from George.

Sally and Judy may have shunned the media spotlight, but they seemed to be getting the best tasks. The robotic arm was turning into a vital system for mission specialists, with its ability to move objects in space and to take photographs with a camera inside its tip, and Sally and Judy had become masters of it. Anna had also started work on the robotic arm and had become just as good at controlling it.

One big assignment pushed Sally ahead of the pack. She was named as a Capsule Communicator, or CAPCOM, for STS-2 and STS-3, the second and third flights of the shuttle. A CAPCOM relayed important communication over the radio to the astronauts in space. As CAPCOM, Sally served as a link between the crew and the dozens of people in Mission Control. She was the first of the Six to be given this role, although Judy was also present in Mission Control for STS-3 as the go-to robotic arm expert.

There was just no way to predict who would get the nod, and by early 1982 still no announcement had been made.

By then Rhea had become pregnant, so she figured she was out of the running. She knew that having a baby was probably going to push back her flight assignments. "I had to decide: Do I want to have a baby now and be delayed in getting a flight? Or do I want to get a lot of flights and then try to have a baby? And I wasn't terribly young anymore," she said later. "So, to me, it was just more important to have a baby—to have children and maybe never get a flight."

And Hoot told her something important: "I think later on in life you'll be just as happy that you got to fly, but that you weren't the first." It would be years before she understood the power of those words. Being first wasn't always going to be wonderful.

Whoever was chosen to fly, the seventh mission, STS-7, was going to make history another way by doing something new. In addition to putting two telecommunications satellites into orbit, the astronauts were going to use the robotic arm to grab on to an object in the payload bay, place it in orbit, and then grab it again and return it to the bay. This would require a lot of precision in operating the robotic arm and also in flying the shuttle, which would have to maneuver delicately in space.

For commander of that mission George wanted Bob Crippen, who'd flown on the shuttle's first mission. George felt he was ready to lead one. He then chose Rick Hauck as the pilot. But who would be the two mission specialists?

George chose John Fabian as one of them. He'd been the head of robotic arm training at one point. Both Sally and Judy had worked closely with John, and he'd given each of them a glowing review. But only one would go up.

George decided on Sally. He also wanted Guion Bluford as a mission specialist on the following flight, STS-8. The first woman and first Black American flying back-to-back missions would be groundbreaking for the space program—and for the United States.

First, though, George had to sell Chris Kraft on his choices. To George's surprise, Chris felt that there were at least two women better qualified than Sally for STS-7, but George convinced him that Sally had the right mix of skills, experience, and personality.

Bob agreed. "We all knew that whoever was going to be the first woman to fly was going to get more attention than they'd probably ever want," he later recalled. "And so we wanted somebody that we thought could handle all that—that was good under pressure." He had flown and worked with Sally and thought she could manage it. He also felt that Sally, as an introvert, wasn't one to seek the spotlight or fame. He and George agreed that they didn't want to choose someone who wanted the attention too badly or would let it go to their head. Knowing that Sally had worked a lot with John, Bob was confident the crew would get along during training and in space.

But to convince Chris, George needed more than gut feelings. So he made a spreadsheet, putting Xs next to each candidate's skills. A quick glance showed Sally and Judy tied, with Anna not far behind. But in the end Sally had one more X—she had a better understanding of more systems than the others. She was truly the most qualified. A few days later Chris finally accepted Sally and the other assignments.

Early on Monday morning, April 19, 1982, Sally was summoned to George's office. He asked how she liked her CAPCOM duties. "We thought that maybe you enjoyed what you were doing so much that maybe you wouldn't want to fly on a crew," he said.

Sally made it crystal clear: she was very interested in flying on a crew. Without saying much more, George took Sally to Chris Kraft's office.

The director launched into a speech about what this assignment would mean. It was going to be a difficult few months and years. The job would come with responsibilities beyond the actual mission. Had Sally thought long and hard about what accepting it would mean? The lights of the combined American media focused squarely on her? The questions?

Sally understood that he was giving her an out, but it's against the nature of an astronaut to turn down an open seat on a spacecraft. "There was no doubt in my mind that I wanted to do that," Sally said. She was ready.

That afternoon, at an informal meeting of the astronauts, George said, "We've made some crew assignments," and then read out the names of those who would fly on the seventh, eighth, and ninth missions. Knowing that he'd just broken the hearts of most of the people in the room, he added, "Hopefully we'll get more people assigned soon."

The mood instantly changed, and a split formed in the TFNG class, separating those with crew assignments from the rest. While the unassigned astronauts smiled and congratulated their lucky peers, many felt jealousy and disappointment eating away inside. Watching their classmates celebrate but not knowing when they might go into space was excruciating.

For the Six the unspoken competition had officially come to an end. Sally would be the One. Her name would resound through history. And in addition to the obvious perks that would come with being the first American woman in space, Sally would get to fly before the others.

For Judy, Anna, and Kathy, the news came as a blow. "I would have loved to have gone first," Kathy said. "I was confident in my abilities."

"Of course, every one of us wanted to be first, but then that's true of everybody in their class—for the guys, too," Anna said. "That's just the nature of the competitive group of people that have basically been competing their whole lives."

For Shannon, who wasn't so caught up in being first, the tough part was the waiting. She just wanted to see space— she'd wanted it her whole life. When you're an astronaut, and your sole ambition is to fly, it stings knowing that you still have many months or even years to wait.

Sally did her best to be outwardly humble but shared her excitement with Steve. When she talked to Steve about the assignment, her joy revolved around the fact that she had crewmates—all friends of hers—and that she got to start training as soon as possible. He noticed that she didn't seem to acknowledge the meaning of being first. He wondered if she fully understood the amount of pressure she would feel in the years to come.

A week after Sally and her crewmates got their assignments, the media showed up at the space center for a press conference with them. Wearing a purple blouse, Sally sat on the stage behind a conference table with the other three who would fly STS-7.

"How does it feel to realize," a male reporter asked her, "that because primarily of the luck of your birth, along with some good work and so on, you are going to become a footnote in history and a trivia question subject forever, among other things?"

Everyone in the room laughed, including Sally. Gracefully she answered without a hint of frustration. "Well, of course, I was very honored that NASA chose me to be the first woman. I guess that I was maybe more excited about getting a chance to fly early than I was about getting to be the first woman."

Nearly all the questions at the half-hour press conference revolved around Sally in some way. When the reporters weren't asking Sally a silly question, they were asking it of her colleagues. One wondered if the men would defer to Sally and let her do more tasks out of politeness, like opening the door for a woman here on Earth. "I don't think that Dr. Ride needs anybody in any group to defer to her," John Fabian replied. "I think that her capabilities take care of themselves and she'll stand high in any group."

Standing out among all the questions, though, was *the* question. The one Sally would be asked for the rest of her life. *How does it feel?*

"I'm sure you've been asked many times how it feels to be the first woman astronaut. . . . How does it feel to be asked that question?" one reporter asked. "How do you respond to that question?"

"I've also been asked many times how it feels to be asked that question," Sally said, as the room laughed. "I think that I'm going to get real tired of that question."

There was no time to dwell on that question or any other, however, because Sally's training for the flight began at once. The entire crew of STS-7 moved into John Fabian's former office and got to work. They mapped out the flight plan and the payloads. Sally's robotic arm skills had been key in getting her on the crew, and she had to keep them sharp, which meant lots of training sessions.

But Sally would also be the mission's flight engineer, a critical rank that made her the backup to commander Bob and pilot Rick. Sally would sit just behind those two during the ascent to space and the return trip home. If something went wrong, she'd help with the checklist or monitor the displays, so that Bob and Rick could focus on saving the crew. She spent plenty of time in the simulators with Bob and Rick, practicing the ascent and reentry over and over and over again.

Being flight engineer also meant that Sally would have a fantastic view during the climb to space. She'd see the windows and control panel between the pilot and the commander. She'd watch the thick blue atmosphere of Earth fade into the black of space.

A few months into training, Sally realized there was something she wanted to do before liftoff. She and Steve traveled to Kansas to Steve's parents' house. They'd been there many times before, but this time Sally's sister, Karen, nicknamed Bear, was there. Steve's father and Bear, a Presbyterian minister, co-officiated at Sally and Steve's backyard wedding.

It was a small affair, something that came as a bit of a surprise to everyone—even Steve. Leading up to the wedding, he and Sally often didn't see much of each other. With their hectic work schedules, they seemed like two ships passing in the night. "It didn't seem like I was a real priority," Steve would later say, looking back. "And, in fact, I was going to suggest: why don't we go separately from here on out." But as he prepared to suggest that, Sally shocked him by saying that her feelings for him were quite strong. He loved her, even if he felt that his feelings were stronger than hers, so they continued dating. Then one day Sally casually suggested getting married.

"I knew back then, and it became even clearer later, that she was pretty much going to do what she wanted to do," he said later. "And in terms of our relationship, I guess I decided that was okay with me. However she wanted to play it was fine." The two exchanged vows in T-shirts and white jeans. Keeping their wedding low-key meant that it earned only a short paragraph in the newspapers.

Just as Sally and Steve began a new chapter in their lives, so did Rhea and Hoot. Their son, Paul Seddon Gibson, was born. Alarmingly, the newborn needed swift emergency care to help him breathe. The next few days were painfully anxious, until he started breathing on his own. Rhea and Hoot eventually presented their healthy baby to the press during a conference arranged by NASA. Everyone wanted to get a glimpse of the world's first "astrotot," the child of two astronauts. But Paul wouldn't be the only one for long.

At that point Anna was thirty-three and Bill was thirty-six. Their flight assignments were taking much longer than they had expected. When the TFNGs had started the astronaut program, they'd been told they would be flying within three years. Now, nearly five years later, Anna still didn't know where she stood in the flight lineup. But she did know that she was ready to have a child. Months later Anna learned that she was pregnant. Like Rhea, she continued to work as long as possible.

The First Pregnant Astronauts

How would NASA react when a woman astronaut became pregnant? Rhea found out in early 1982.

At that time the Six were waiting anxiously to learn which of them would be the first American woman in space, but Rhea had discovered she was pregnant late in 1981. While she and Hoot privately celebrated, they agreed not to tell NASA right away. Rhea feared that NASA managers would ban her from parts of her training, especially from flying in the high-speed, high-altitude T-38 jets, so she began a research project of her own. Combining the caution of a medical doctor with the undercover skills of a spy, she gathered as much information as possible. When the time came to reveal her pregnancy, she wanted to present NASA with evidence: *I'm pregnant, and I can still safely fly.*

By March 1982, Rhea's baby bump was getting too big to easily conceal, so she and Hoot talked to the astronauts' upper management. Rhea made it clear that she didn't plan to quit working, including doing her job as a helicopter doctor for the upcoming third shuttle mission.

After the meetings Rhea returned to her office, content with how they had gone. Nobody had freaked out or said no. But as soon as she sat down, her phone rang. The caller was one of the space centers' flight surgeons, telling her she was no longer allowed to fly in the T-38 while she was pregnant.

Shocked, Rhea tried to explain that she'd gathered data on the subject and felt she'd be all right. The surgeon didn't want to hear the data. The simple truth was that NASA didn't want to risk bad publicity if something went wrong with her pregnancy during a flight. When Rhea asked how she was supposed to get to California to perform as a helicopter doctor, the surgeon said, "Fly commercial." Case closed.

Rhea felt dizzy as she hung up the phone. This was exactly the kind of response she'd dreaded. NASA was still run by men—men of a much older generation—and their idea of what a pregnant woman could handle was outdated. But Rhea knew that fighting back was out of the question, because she might be seen as "difficult." So she held her head up and went back to work.

When Anna later learned that she was pregnant, she also decided to keep it a secret from NASA as long as she could. She had seen what had happened to Rhea, and she didn't want to be grounded from the T-38s.

Keeping silent turned out to be harder than Anna had expected, though. For one mission she was assigned to strap in the crew before they launched. Easy enough—but the assignment also meant she had to prepare for emergencies. If something happened to the crew, she had to haul them out of the cockpit. NASA wanted to test her ability to do that. It was always going to be a struggle for petite Anna to carry two-hundred-pound, six-foot-tall men out into the Florida heat. And now she was secretly four months pregnant too.

"Anna, if you do that, I'm going to shoot you," a concerned Bill told his wife.

"Bill, if you can think of a way for me to get out of it without telling them I'm pregnant, fine," Anna replied. "Otherwise, I'm going to do it."

And she did do it. It was tough, but Anna got through it with no complications, although a female suit technician working alongside her mentioned Anna's baby bump to her team afterward. Not long after that, Anna and Bill broke the news of the pregnancy to NASA and their fellow astronauts.

As 1983 began, Sally's training became busier and more complex. And George had assigned another TFNG, Norm Thagard, to the mission. STS-7 would now have a crew of five.

A medical doctor by training, Norm would investigate a problem that had existed since human spaceflight had begun: Space Adaptation Syndrome (SAS). More than half the people NASA sent into space got unbelievably nauseous and vomited as soon as they got into orbit. It struck at random. Seasoned pilots would feel their stomachs churning. Mission specialists who didn't even ride roller coasters on the ground could float vomit-free in microgravity. Norm would develop experiments to determine who got sick, why—and how to prevent it.

Meanwhile, Sally and the other STS-7 astronauts spent a lot of time in the shuttle simulators, where Sally and John traded off working with the robotic arm. Every punch of the joystick, every push of a button had to be second nature in space.

Over time the simulations grew to last for up to fifty-six hours. They involved not just the crew but many engineers and flight controllers in Mission Control. The simulation supervisors were always ready to mix up a cocktail of glitches and malfunctions that could tear apart the mission. Each time, Sally and her team raced to fix the problem before their virtual shuttle fell to its doom.

On one day Sally had to do bench checks, which meant reviewing the personal items she wanted to take to space. This time the engineers wanted her to look over some other items that had been laid out for her. One was a personal hygiene kit created by NASA engineers. These kits had been around since the early Gemini flights. They included basic grooming supplies such as a toothbrush. Now, though, NASA had made a kit geared toward women. Nestled inside it was a smaller kit wrapped in yellow plastic.

It was a makeup kit.

To Sally the idea of even thinking about wearing

makeup in space felt like a joke. "A makeup kit brought to you by NASA engineers," she said, then added, "You can just imagine the discussions among the predominantly male engineers about what should go in a makeup kit." She looked around for an ally. Luckily, she ran into Kathy. The two did their best to approve the hygiene and makeup kits, even though it was the last thing they wanted to do.

Kathy and Sally might have rolled their eyes, but not everyone felt the same. Just like women in any profession, the Six were individuals with their own opinions and their own ways of being a woman astronaut. Rhea, for one, approved of the makeup kit. "If there would be pictures taken of me from space, I didn't want to fade into the background, so I requested some basic items," she said later.

While reviewing the products, Sally noticed a weird band of pink plastic. She tugged it gently out of the hygiene kit. Out came a tampon. And then another. And another. The engineers present at the bench check asked Sally if one hundred would be the right number of tampons for her weeklong trip, as Sally and Kathy stifled their laughter.

"No. That would not be the right number," Sally replied calmly.

"Well, we want to be safe."

"Well, you can cut that in half with no problem at all," said Sally, while Kathy broke up into giggles. Of course it was considerate to provide products for monthly periods to women going into space, but the extreme oversupply was a comical sign of how little most men at the time knew about the facts of women's lives.

To guard Sally from overwhelming press attention during her training, NASA often used her busy schedule as an excuse to turn down media opportunities. When Sally did speak to reporters on behalf of the mission, she had at least one other member of the crew with her, if not the whole crew. But the press wanted more of Sally, so to satisfy the public's thirst for knowledge, she agreed to talk to a reporter from the *Washington Post* for a detailed series of articles. That reporter happened to be Sue Okie, her childhood friend.

To Sally, Sue didn't feel like a journalist. She was just Sue, and Sally felt at ease talking to her longtime friend for hours on end. A few years earlier, though, a question from Sue had reminded Sally of the price of being a public figure.

Sue had heard from a sports reporter that Sally and her college roommate, Molly, had been a "lesbian couple." This was news to Sue, who wanted to get confirmation directly from her friend. She went to New York to see Sally, who was giving a speech. Afterward, when the two were alone, Sue built up the courage to ask. Had Sally and Molly been in a romantic relationship?

After a pause Sally said, "No. Molly wanted that, but I didn't." Sue never brought it up again. But Sally had been shocked and worried by the question. Who had told Sue? Sally was an intensely private person who didn't like to share even the most ordinary parts of her life. She had always wanted to keep her relationship with Molly completely private. Now she was angry at the thought that the world might find out about it.

Attitudes about gay couples were changing in the early 1980s, but not fast enough. In 1981, Sally's tennis idol, Billie Jean King, came out about her relationship with another woman. The reaction was swift. The press showed some support, but within twenty-four hours the tennis star had lost all her endorsements, a major part of a top athlete's income.

Sally could only imagine what would happen if her relationship with Molly surfaced in the news. But time passed, and no rumors arose. Eventually Sally was too busy to worry. She trusted Sue not to reveal anything too private, so in the months just before her flight, Sally met with Sue in Houston to go over her life and training.

Sue watched in awe as her high school friend, the former slacker, studied mission manuals and flight books deep into the night. "I have lost my dominant trait, which has been not to work at things," Sally told her. "I'm really working hard, and I have been for three years. And I enjoy it. In fact, I'm obsessed with it."

Sue also saw Sally and her crew in the simulator, battling the failures thrown at them. During one training

The Six gather around the "personal rescue sphere." During the selection process, all the women had to curl up in the sphere to prove they weren't prone to claustrophobia.
NASA/INTERIM ARCHIVES/
GETTY IMAGES

All astronaut candidates who weren't jet pilots had to undergo water survival training in Florida. Anna Fisher and Sally Ride can be seen sitting on the dock, waiting their turn to be pulled into the air by a helicopter.
KEN HAWKINS/ALAMY
STOCK PHOTO

From left: Sally Ride, Judy Resnik, Anna Fisher, Kathy Sullivan, and Rhea Seddon pose at Homestead Air Force Base during water survival training.
SPACE FRONTIERS/
ARCHIVE PHOTOS/
GETTY IMAGES

LEFT: This photo, taken of Anna Fisher during a space-suit fitting, became iconic.

JOHN BRYSON/SYGMA VIA GETTY IMAGES

BELOW: Kathy Sullivan stands before the nose cone of a WB-57F reconnaissance aircraft at Ellington Field Joint Reserve Base on July 1, 1979. She'd go on to set an unofficial altitude record for women in it, reaching an altitude of 63,300 feet.

SPACE FRONTIERS/ARCHIVE PHOTOS/ HULTON ARCHIVE/GETTY IMAGES

LEFT: Sally Ride climbs into a T-38 jet. Mission specialists like Sally flew in the back seat with pilots in the front, but each of the Six learned how to fly and land the fighters themselves.

NASA/AFP VIA GETTY IMAGES

In the foreground, George Abbey (center) stands next to STS-1 crewmember Bob Crippen (left) and astronaut Joe Engle (right) at NASA's Kennedy Space Center in Florida on April 11, 1981.

NASA

Sally Ride and Anna Fisher work together at Kennedy Space Center on the payloads for Sally's flight STS-7. Anna is visibly pregnant with her first daughter, Kristin.

NASA PHOTO SCANNED BY J. L. PICKERING

The new space shuttle *Discovery* is transported to its launch site in Cape Canaveral, Florida, on the back of a modified Boeing 747. *Discovery*'s first flight to space would be Judy Resnik's first flight.

NASA PHOTO SCANNED BY J. L. PICKERING

LEFT: The crew of STS-41-D poses for a photo mid-flight. Pictured clockwise from Judy Resnik are Steve Hawley, Mike Coats, Henry "Hank" Hartsfield, Mike Mullane, and Charlie Walker.

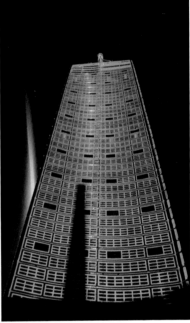

ABOVE: The unfurled solar array carried on STS-41-D. Judy Resnik was in charge of the experiment while on board.

LEFT: Kathy Sullivan in her flight suit, undergoing preflight checks.

Kathy Sullivan and Dave Leestma perform the orbital refueling system experiment during a spacewalk on STS-41-G.
NASA PHOTO SCANNED BY J. L. PICKERING

Astronaut Dale Gardner holds up a "For Sale" sign during STS-51-A, after he and Joe Allen successfully retrieved two stranded satellites in space. Anna Fisher aided the recovery while working the robotic arm.
NASA PHOTO SCANNED BY
J. L. PICKERING

Anna Fisher is reunited with her husband, Bill, and daughter, Kristin, after returning from space.
NASA PHOTO SCANNED BY
J. L. PICKERING

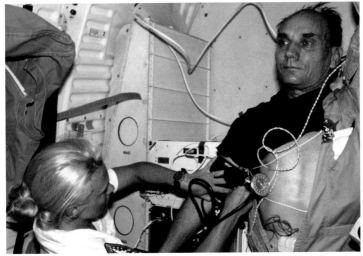

Rhea Seddon performs a medical experiment on Senator Jake Garn during STS-51-D.

The crew of STS-51-D pose with the "lacrosse stick" and "flyswatter." Clockwise from the top left is Jake Garn, Donald Williams, Karol "Bo" Bobko, Charlie Walker, Dave Walker, Rhea Seddon, and Jeff Hoffman.

Rhea Seddon is reunited with her three-year-old son, Paul, after returning to Houston.

LEFT: Shannon Lucid floats near the cockpit during her flight STS-51-G.
NASA PHOTO SCANNED BY J. L. PICKERING

ABOVE: Before their flight, Judy Resnik poses with her crewmate Christa McAuliffe who was set to become the first teacher to fly to space.
NASA PHOTO SCANNED BY J. L. PICKERING

LEFT: Prior to the launch of STS-51-L, the extremely cold weather caused icicles to form on the launchpad structure, leading to concerns that the ice could break and damage the Space Shuttle during launch.
NASA PHOTO SCANNED BY J. L. PICKERING

At 73 seconds after launch, a "major malfunction" occurred during STS-51-L. The accident led to the deaths of all seven crew members on board, including Judy Resnik. NASA PHOTO SCANNED BY J. L. PICKERING

The remains of the *Challenger* crew members are transferred from seven hearses to a transport plane at Kennedy Space Center. NASA PHOTO SCANNED BY J. L. PICKERING

Sally Ride's life partner, Tam O'Shaughnessy, accepts the 2013 Presidential Medal of Freedom on behalf of Sally, who died of pancreatic cancer on July 23, 2012. LEIGH VOGEL/WIREIMAGE

run the crew did everything they possibly could to overcome the swarm of virtual failures. The space shuttle still
"crashed," virtually killing them all.

That moment shocked Sue. It was a wake-up call that
spaceflight wasn't a risk-free enterprise. But Sally, as was her
way, didn't betray any fear at all. She and the others would
shrug off a crash and vow to do better on the next run.
"They can always give you enough failures that the plane
will crash," Bob Crippen told the stunned Sue.

Sue's stories ran for four days in the *Washington Post*,
but that didn't satisfy the country's curiosity. "It seems my
life isn't my own anymore," Sally said. Her smiling face
appeared on many magazine covers, and inside were stories
written by journalists who'd tried their best to pry information out of Sally and her family. As her sister, Bear, told
Newsweek, "She doesn't offer information. . . . If you want
to know something about Sally, you have to ask her." A
Los Angeles Times article said that reporters found her "difficult, unreachable, stone-cold, in contempt of the press."
But Sally just refused to play all their games.

Her skill at giving calm answers and turning away
unwanted questions, though, was tested on May 24, 1983.
It was a standard press conference like those held before
every shuttle launch, but this time the large gaggle of
reporters had Sally in their sights.

Sally set the tone from the start. The same reporter

who'd asked her at the previous press conference what it felt like to become a footnote in history asked her feelings about it again.

"I guess that my answer is probably going to be the same as it was a year ago," Sally replied. "I'm so excited to get a chance to fly that I'm able to ignore all you people."

The room laughed, and the battle had officially begun. The American press still seemed to be extremely confused how this whole woman-in-space thing was going to work, and they were determined to ask Sally every manner of question about it, from living in tight quarters with men to whether the men deferred to her or gave her special treatment in any way.

When a woman reporter asked if Sally planned to be the first mother in space, she pointedly didn't answer. She might not have mastered slamming tennis balls over the net as well as she liked, but Sally had certainly mastered how to smack each reporter's question back at them with equal speed. And her crewmates became just as skilled at this verbal volley.

"We've interviewed lots of Texans this week," one reporter told the crew. "And they don't think women should be astronauts."

"What kinds of Texans did you talk to?" Bob Crippen snapped back.

"You know, those guys with the big hats," the reporter said.

"Well, I'm a native Texan," said Bob. "I wear a big hat, and I drive a pickup truck, and I think I disagree with those guys in the big hats. I think it's great that there are women astronauts, and I think it's great that Sally Ride is making this flight."

But the press kept going. When one reporter asked her if she ever wept when encountering a glitch in the simulator, her face practically screamed what she couldn't say out loud herself: *You cannot be serious.* Again she was forced to laugh it off, joking, "Why doesn't anybody ask Rick those questions?" Although the room laughed, Sally had pointed out something important—how differently the media approached questioning her.

Eventually Sally got a moment to sum up how she felt about all the attention and the trivial or sexist questions. "It's too bad that our society isn't further along and that this is such a big deal," she said. "But I guess if the American public thinks that it's a big deal, then it's probably good that it's getting the coverage that it's getting. I think it's time we get away from that, and it's time people realized that women in this country can do any job they want to do."

A week before her flight Sally finally escaped from the clamor of the media. The STS-7 crew entered quarantine in a trailer inside a JSC building. And three days before the scheduled liftoff, Sally climbed into the back of a T-38 and jetted east to meet the space shuttle *Challenger*, waiting for her at the Cape.

The time of waiting and training was over.

The Race Isn't Over

America had won the race to be first on the moon, but the space race wasn't entirely over. The Soviet Union still wanted to beat the United States in other ways if it could.

On August 19, 1982, exactly four months after NASA had announced that Sally Ride would be the first American woman in space, another milestone in space history was about to happen, directed by the Soviet Union's space agency. At the agency's spaceport in the central Asian nation of Kazakhstan, a rocket topped by a cosmonaut capsule stood on a launchpad. A red-haired woman in a Soviet space suit climbed in.

Svetlana Savitskaya, not Sally Ride, became the second woman in the world to fly to space.

When the Soviet Union had learned that NASA was going to add nonmilitary people to its astronaut corps, the Soviets had begun recruiting more cosmonauts, including women. So when NASA announced Sally's assignment to fly, the

Soviets were determined to fly another woman cosmonaut first.

Nineteen years after Valentina Tereshkova had become the first woman in space, Svetlana reached orbit and docked with a Soviet space station called Salyut 7—another space race milestone that the United States had not yet achieved. Two cosmonauts were already living aboard Salyut. When Svetlana arrived, they presented her with flowers that had been grown in orbit.

And when the three had their first meal together, they presented her with an apron. "There is a kitchen and that will be where you work," cosmonaut Valentin Lebedev joked. It was supposedly a piece of lighthearted humor, but it showed that no matter what women accomplished, traditional ideas about gender roles were still alive in the Soviet Union, just as in the United States.

As for Sally, she barely registered the fact that Svetlana's flight demoted her from second to third woman in space. She was too busy training.

CHAPTER FIFTEEN
Sally's Ride

★ ★ ★ ★ ★ ★

S ally invited nearly everyone she knew to the launch. The Ride family crossed from the West Coast to the East Coast. So did plenty of Sally's tennis buddies, including Tam O'Shaughnessy. The two had stayed in touch on and off since their days dancing to records after tennis matches. Two of Sally's previous partners were also there: Bill Colson, who'd been with Sally when she'd started at NASA, and Molly Tyson, whom the world knew only as Sally's former roommate and close friend.

Sally didn't get to interact with most of her guests, though. The biggest irony of inviting someone to see you fly on the space shuttle was that you didn't get to see them before you flew. Sally and her crewmates were in quarantine before the flight, to prevent them from catching a nasty bug and taking it to orbit. But George Abbey sensed that Sally was feeling nervous. Thinking a quick visit from a friend might be good for her, he had Molly undergo a physical so she could see Sally on the evening before launch. Sally was pleasantly surprised by the visit.

They talked about unimportant things. Molly noticed that her friend seemed particularly upbeat, ready to charge into the ring. But as Molly got up to leave, Sally showed a rare moment of vulnerability. "I'm aware that this is not without risks," Sally told her friend, suddenly serious. "I realize I could die."

In that moment Molly understood that the legendary Sally Ride—the woman she'd always seen as some kind of godlike figure—could get scared too. The two never spoke about that conversation again.

The next day started with a wake-up call at 3:13 a.m. Sally tried to act like a normal person as she trotted out to eat the traditional pre-launch breakfast with her crewmates. Video cameras captured every bite. "I was struggling very hard . . . trying to look like nothing unusual was about to happen to us," Sally recalled. After eating, she slipped into the sky-blue, long-sleeved jumpsuit she'd wear for flight.

When the crew drove out to the launchpad, they first dropped George Abbey off at the Launch Control Center, a squat concrete building with windows angled to the sky. Since the Apollo program, it had served as the central hub for monitoring human spaceflight missions from the Cape. On this early morning the center buzzed with energy and excitement as everyone inside prepared for the coming launch.

As they continued toward the shuttle, Commander Bob

Crippen turned to his crew. "That's the last one of those," he said, referring to the officials they'd left behind. "All the sane people are back there. We're the only people crazy enough to go out here." Then, alone with their thoughts, the crew got into an elevator at the launchpad's base for the ride to the cockpit.

On the beaches a few miles away, half a million people waited to see the launch, vibrating with anticipation. But Sally was blissfully unaware of the hordes of gawkers. In the few hours before launch, as NASA's countdown clock ticked toward zero, the shuttle's cockpit was her entire world. Lying on her metal seat, she stared ahead at the control panel and screens that filled her view between the pilot and commander seats.

T-minus thirty seconds. . . .

NASA's flight controllers handed control of *Challenger* over to the vehicle's computers. The shuttle was now in charge. If anything went wrong, its computers would have to stop the flight. Almost in slow motion the seconds fell away.

T-minus ten seconds. . . .

Sally could feel the slightest bump in her heart rate, but she stayed cool, focused on the moment that would completely change her life.

T-minus six seconds. . . .

A deafening roar broke the silence. *Challenger*'s three

main engines had ignited, sending intense vibrations up through the cockpit. It was almost time to break free.

"We have ignition!" Bob Crippen called out to his crew. And then: "We have liftoff!"

In that moment Sally knew she was no longer in the driver's seat of her life. "All of a sudden, I felt totally helpless, totally overwhelmed by what was happening there," she said later. "It was just very, very clear that for the next several seconds, we had absolutely no control over our fates." Sally surrendered herself to *Challenger* as it burst through the clouds, rolled onto its back, and took a glorious swan dive into the sky.

But Sally still had a job to do. Her main task during ascent was to keep an eye on the checklist attached to her knee. As each milestone event of the flight happened, she would call them out. She had trained over and over for this, but blasting into space was a profoundly intense experience. It took all of her strength to make her first callout just a few seconds into launch. She squeaked out, "LV, LH," an acronym that meant the shuttle was correctly positioned in the sky. "I'll guarantee that those were the hardest words I ever had to get out of my mouth," Sally said later.

Shuddering violently, with its booster rockets firing, *Challenger* pierced through the atmosphere. The crew were jostled as they clung to their seats. But when the rockets separated from the shuttle as planned, the violent shaking disappeared. The ride became as smooth as if *Challenger* were gliding on invisible tracks to space. Its engines drove them the rest of the way into orbit, then shut down.

"We have MECO," Mission Control said, referring to main engine cutoff.

And all at once the astronauts were floating. Sally took the checklist from her knee and released it into the air in front of her. It didn't fall. Next to her John whooped loudly in celebration.

They were in space.

Sally stayed strapped to her seat, waiting for the last few milestones she would call out. A loud clang meant that the external fuel tank was breaking away to fall back toward Earth. Then the shuttle's thrusters fired the last few burns to put them into their planned orbit.

Once those burns were done, Sally pushed herself out of her metal chair for her first look out the windows at the miraculous view. From nearly two hundred miles up, the crew watched as Africa passed below them. They had crossed the Atlantic Ocean in just eight minutes.

After Bob confirmed to Mission Control that the crew was in good spirits, Sally got hold of the radio for a few seconds to describe her experience.

"Ever been to Disneyland?" Sally asked Houston over the intercom.

"Affirmative," the mission's CAPCOM replied.

"That was definitely an E ticket," said Sally, referring to the type of ticket that once got the park's visitors onto the newest, biggest, and most advanced rides.

"Roger that, Sally."

Before the mission Sally had said that her biggest worry was that she would somehow mess up. What she didn't say was something that the Six had all grappled with: just one mistake, no matter how small, had big consequences. If Sally couldn't get it right in space, the people who were critical or unsure about women astronauts would think that *all* women would fall short.

Fortunately for future generations of women spacefarers, Sally did as well as NASA and George Abbey had expected. It took some time, though, to get used to working in the weightlessness of microgravity.

The first day in orbit, she felt clumsy and inefficient. The first couple of meals were a pain. She couldn't anchor herself down properly and relax while eating. Later she'd talk about the "real steep learning curve towards figuring out how to operate" in orbit. She also had to fight the urge to drift off to sleep—spaceflight sometimes comes with unexplained tiredness. But after a few days Sally adapted and took to microgravity with ease. She felt no nausea, though she had a "pitching" sensation whenever she looked out the window and saw Earth streaming by beneath her.

The crew crossed off some major items on their to-do list. In the first two days, they released the communications satellites into the void. Both bus-sized satellites twirled out into space just as planned.

Then it was time to have some fun.

One of the main reasons why Sally had been chosen for the mission was to conduct demonstrations of the robotic arm with an experimental payload labeled SPAS-01. She and John would use their robotic arm skills to put the experimental payload into space, then back into the shuttle. John took the first shift. He extended the arm out into space and positioned it above the cargo hold. It looked like the claw of an arcade game ready to snag a prize. He lowered the arm, plucked SPAS-01 out of its cradle, and pulled it up and out of the bay.

As if placing a book on a shelf, John dragged the arm out into space and released SPAS-01. With the payload free it was time for the shuttle's orbital dance. Bob piloted *Challenger* down and away from the SPAS-01, then rotated the shuttle so that its open hold was under the free-flying satellite.

It was a perfect photo op. The result was a dark, moody photograph of the shuttle against the backdrop of a vivid blue ocean, sprinkled with snowy-white clouds. Then John used the arm again to take hold of the satellite.

After lunch it was Sally's turn. She steered the arm with

SPAS-01 attached, dragging the satellite out into space and leaving it on its own. Sally then had to move the arm out of the way so that Rick could pilot *Challenger* around the satellite, practicing a different maneuver.

During their demonstrations Sally and John captured images of the work they'd trained so hard for. At one point they bent the robotic arm so that it looked like the number seven, for their mission, STS-7. "Those pictures are a very important part of my memory of the flight," John said years later.

Finally it was time to tuck SPAS-01 back into its cradle inside the shuttle. One last time Sally controlled the arm. As she made her crucial maneuver, uncertainty gripped her. *This is real metal that will hit real metal if I miss,* she thought. *What if we don't capture this satellite?*

But she'd trained hundreds of hours for this moment. And she didn't miss. She neatly stowed SPAS-01, and their biggest job was complete.

It was a fairly flawless mission—save for one scary moment when Rick noticed a small crack in the space shuttle's windshield. A small particle had penetrated partly into the windowpane. Fortunately, it hadn't passed all the way through. If the hole had been any bigger or deeper, the crew could have been killed instantly.

The crew decided to keep an eye on the tiny blemish and not tell Mission Control about it, figuring it would just worry the engineers. (Bob would get in a spot of trouble for that decision.) Later they'd learn that a tiny fleck of paint had likely hit the windshield and caused a little crater. The smallest thing can hit hard when moving at 17,500 miles per hour!

At night or in the early morning hours, the astronauts took turns staring out the shuttle's windows. "I never got tired of looking out the window at Earth," Sally said later. "It's just a constantly changing view, and it's just a beautiful sight."

One moment coral reefs peeked out at her from under the turquoise waters surrounding Australia. The next, a massive orange dust storm appeared over northern Africa, crawling slowly across the continent. Gargantuan white cyclones swirled over the oceans. "It was just a spectacular feeling to be able to look down at the moon's reflection along rivers and watch our progress up the east coast of the US," Sally said.

But what stood out to her most was Earth's atmosphere and its stark contrast with the blackness of space. "It looked as if someone had taken a royal-blue crayon and just traced along Earth's horizon," she said. "And then I realized that that blue line—that really thin royal-blue line—was Earth's atmosphere. And that was all there was of it."

In those moments, Sally realized just how fragile life is. From nearly two hundred miles up, the air that keeps all of humanity alive looks like nothing more than a fuzzy thin band surrounding Earth's outer edge. The sight made her more aware than ever of the importance of keeping that atmosphere intact for generations to come.

During Sally's six days in space, she did her job and tried to ignore any history that was being made, though STS-7 was bursting with historic firsts, such as when Mary Cleave called up to give Sally instructions for a small adjustment to the shuttle's computer. It was the first time a woman on Earth had spoken to a woman in space. Although one reporter lamented how ordinary the conversation was for such a remarkable occasion, that didn't register at all for Sally or Mary. They were doing their jobs.

One first didn't happen, though. STS-7 was scheduled to make the first shuttle landing in Florida. On the day of reentry, however, a thick fogbank rolled over NASA's brand-new landing strip there, forcing Sally and the others to land at Edwards Air Force Base in California, as all the earlier missions had done. Bob and Rick steered the shuttle out of orbit, sending the vehicle on its dive toward Earth. During the descent Sally watched the bright glow of the atmosphere heat up around the shuttle.

For Sally the unexpected detour was a blessing in disguise. She landed 2,500 miles from the thousands of people who'd gathered at Cape Canaveral to see her arrive. Only a small crowd of air force personnel and their families were on hand at Edwards to greet the STS-7 crew. Sally told them, "The thing that I'll remember most about that flight is that it was fun. And in fact, I'm sure it's the most fun I'll ever have in my life."

Fun gave way to a new reality almost as soon as Sally returned to Houston.

Someone at the airport handed Sally a giant bouquet of white roses with a large bow while she was on her way home. She lugged it to the Johnson Space Center, where a crowd had gathered.

As the five crewmates and their spouses prepared to greet the crowd, Sally handed the bouquet to a NASA officer so that her hands would be free. With an arm around Steve she spoke to the cheering crowd. Afterward the officer tried to give the bouquet back to her, but she turned away to talk with George Abbey.

She had no idea of the controversy she was igniting.

A newspaper writer interpreted her simple action as a feminist statement. Soon letters were pouring in. She'd later write, "That one little action—giving back the flowers— probably touched off more mail to me than anything [else] I ever did or said as an astronaut."

The controversy was a sign of what was to come. All eyes were on Sally now. Back from space, with no new mission to train for, she was now even more exposed to the public. Fans wanted to show support. The media wanted to satisfy America's endless curiosity. It was a lot for a private person like Sally to handle.

It began the day she came back to Houston, as crowds of neighbors and news crews gathered outside her and Steve's home. The couple managed to escape and spend the night in another astronaut's house—which led the press to point out that Sally Ride hadn't spent her first night back on Earth in her own home.

In just the first month back, Sally and her fellow crew members sped through appearances in eight states. These included a five-hundred-guest reception at the National Air and Space Museum (where plenty of people wanted Sally's picture and autograph), a military ball, and a White House meal with President Ronald Reagan.

Requests streamed into NASA to book Sally for all kinds of events, big and small. Less than a week after the flight, the agency had more than a thousand requests from the media for her. Some were bizarre, like the artist who wanted Sally to sit for a portrait created out of jelly beans.

Sally's crewmates went with her to as many events as possible, as a buffer between her and the press. Norm Thagard was an actual physical buffer at a press event in Washington, when hordes of TV crews shoved him against the wall to get a shot of Sally.

As the requests kept coming, though, Sally started to feel more and more that her life was out of her control. She was an introvert at heart, but now she seemed to be meeting everyone on the planet. So she pulled away more and more.

It came to a head when NASA pressured her to appear on a television tribute to astronauts hosted by a popular comedian named Bob Hope. Sally turned it down. To her, Bob Hope was a sexist who had a history of parading women in scanty costumes to entertain soldiers. She didn't like his reputation, so she stood firm. When NASA tried to push the issue, she just vanished.

Sally didn't tell anyone where she was going, not even Steve. She'd gone off on her own before, and Steve understood her desire to escape. He didn't think it was particularly responsible of her to do it now, though. After a week she called him. As he'd suspected, she'd gone to California. She had taken refuge with Molly and Molly's partner, making sure that she wouldn't have to appear on that Bob Hope show.

It was dawning on Sally, though, that she needed more than just to get away. She needed some help.

All her life she'd been a happy person, excited to wake up and start each day. Now she woke up nervous, filled with anxiety about what each day might bring. She decided to take care of herself by seeking therapy.

Still, amid the challenges, there were a few moments she cherished. She made multiple appearances on the children's show *Sesame Street*, for example. She loved meeting with the science-curious children. They asked fun questions, such as what it was like to go to the bathroom in space. Sally's fame also meant that she got to meet some of her idols, including feminist Betty Friedan.

But perhaps the most interesting encounter was with someone she'd never expected to meet. She and Steve went to Hungary for an international space conference. At a reception there Sally felt a tap on her elbow. She turned to find Svetlana Savitskaya, the cosmonaut who'd become the second Soviet woman to fly to space in 1982.

"Sally," Svetlana acknowledged.

"Hello," Sally said, cautious.

"Congratulations on your flight."

"Congratulations to you, too," Sally replied.

Their conversation didn't last long. Relations between the United States and the Soviet Union had been especially chilly in recent months. Later that day, though, Sally heard Svetlana talk and decided she was a genuinely good person. Somewhat secretively she arranged a more private meeting with the cosmonaut. A Hungarian physicist she knew helped her get invited to meet a small group of Soviet cosmonauts.

Steve disapproved of the plan. He knew that NASA

took a dim view of American astronauts mingling with Soviet cosmonauts, so he hung back at a coffee shop. Sally, though, was determined.

The mood at first was tense. Neither side knew quite how to act. Sally tried smiling to put everyone at ease, and the cosmonauts immediately made a joke about "no press." The atmosphere eased. Svetlana walked over and sat next to Sally.

The women instantly connected. Svetlana peppered Sally with questions, asking her how long she'd trained and about her flying experience. They swapped stories about their respective spacecraft. Svetlana was fascinated by how the space shuttle landed on a runway. At one point they all laughed about how they slept in space.

Sally really enjoyed talking with Svetlana. "I felt closer to her than I felt to anyone in a very long time," she said. "And it was partly just that I understood a lot of what she had been through." Svetlana, Sally thought, would easily have made it into the astronaut corps in the US. She reminded her a lot of Shannon. Svetlana might have even beaten Sally, if the two had been competing to be the first American woman to orbit Earth.

Sally enjoyed herself so much that she stayed for six hours. Long after midnight she and Svetlana exchanged a few final words and hugged goodbye. "I left with the feeling that we would probably meet again," Sally said. "And if we did, we would be just as close as we were at that moment."

• • •

The whirlwind press tour had brought Sally to unbelievable highs and remarkable lows. In the middle of it all, she sat down with feminist writer Gloria Steinem for an interview. Sally talked about her spaceflight, especially the SPAS-01 demonstration and the pictures taken in space.

"That's probably what our flight will be remembered for, I think, is those pictures," Sally said.

"Want to bet?" Gloria replied.

Bathroom Business

"How do you go to the bathroom in space?" kids at *Sesame Street* asked Sally Ride when she appeared on the show. It was an excellent question. NASA had answered it in several ways over the years—but up until the space shuttle program, only men had gone to the bathroom in space. Because shuttle crews would include women, NASA came up with not one but two new solutions for everyone.

One was the Waste Collection System (WCS), a toilet the astronauts could use in the weightlessness of orbit. It was a very basic throne, with a four-inch hole. The astronauts strapped themselves to the seat, and a system of hoses and bags beneath it collected their waste. The toilet was meant to be used by both men and women, but the Six had to attach a special funnel to the hose to direct their urine the right way. Men can aim their pee. For women, it's not so simple.

Eager to know if the toilet design worked, NASA assigned some of the Six to test it on the Vomit Comet. Before each flight they'd chug as much liquid as they could, filling their bladders to bursting. During their first stint of weightlessness they'd sneak behind a privacy curtain to the toilet and try to relieve themselves into the hose. There was limited success—but plenty of toilet paper was on hand in case some drops escaped and floated away in the weightless environment. After the testers had had their first go, it was time to chug water again. If they were lucky, they could give the throne another try before the end of the flight.

The toilet wasn't a complete answer to the problem of relieving oneself in space. The astronauts also needed something for when they were strapped to their seats for hours, awaiting launch or reentry. Or in case they had to go during a space walk. So NASA engineers created the Disposable Absorption Containment Trunk (DACT). In its most basic form it was a diaper. It was an easy fix in case astronauts had to urinate while out of reach of the toilet. It was designed to absorb solid waste, too, although astronauts probably waited until they reached orbit and could use the WCS for that.

The DACT met the needs of the women astronauts, while the men could still use the devices that the Apollo astronauts had used for peeing inside their flight suits, if they wanted to. Eventually, though, the DACT became standard equipment for all astronauts.

CHAPTER SIXTEEN

Judy's Job

★ ★ ★ ★ ★ ★

Would you have liked to have been the first woman in space?"

Judy had gotten that question often since February 1983. That was when, even before Sally had flown to space, Judy and the world had learned that Judy would be the next American woman to fly. The press seemed obsessed with the question. They thought Judy must have been upset about being in "second place."

She answered with a smile. "I'd like to be *any . . . woman* in space, thank you." It was the perfect answer, but it was also true. Judy just wanted to fly.

Even before Sally had been chosen as the One, Judy had told a reporter, "I'm not here to get my name in the books or to make a name as the first woman astronaut. I'm here to contribute to the space program and do the best job that I can."

But if Judy really had been "somewhat disappointed" not to be first, as her father once told a reporter, her feelings changed when she saw the avalanche of requests that crashed down on Sally after STS-7. To Judy it didn't look like fun.

Judy and Sally shared a dislike for media and publicity, so Judy knew the attention was hard for Sally to bear. "I think Sally did an outstanding job of fielding a difficult situation," Judy told a journalist. "A very bright spotlight was on her as the first one to go, and she handled it very well."

Judy's mission was originally numbered STS-12, meaning that it would be the twelfth shuttle flight. It became STS-41-D when NASA changed its numbering system. Judy couldn't have cared less what the flight was called. All that mattered was that she was going to space.

What's This Mission Called Again?

In the fall of 1983, NASA changed the numbering system for shuttle missions. Up till then the system had been pretty simple: each mission was labeled STS, for "Space Transportation System," followed by the number of that mission's order in flight. But when STS-10's payload was delayed, it meant that STS-11 would be the next to fly. NASA thought the public would have trouble understanding why STS-11 went to space before STS-10, so the agency came up with a wacky new scheme—to *avoid* confusion, they said.

The mission that would have been STS-12 became STS-41-D. The meaning of "STS" remained the same. The number four showed that the flight was set to launch in 1984, and the number one indicated that its planned launch site was Cape Canaveral. As for the *D*, that meant that the mission's payload was the fourth one scheduled for that fiscal year, *D* being the fourth letter of the alphabet.

This was what a less complicated name looked like, according to NASA. But later the astronauts wondered whether the reason for the change was actually superstition, and if NASA had wanted to avoid a mission numbered thirteen, a supposedly unlucky number, especially after Apollo 13 had narrowly avoided disaster during a moon mission back in 1970.

Judy's crewmates would be Hank Hartsfield, an older astronaut who'd flown on the fourth shuttle flight, and three of her TFNG classmates: Mike Coats, Steve Hawley, and Mike Mullane. They'd be the first to fly in a new space shuttle, *Discovery*. Judy already knew some of them well. She'd worked with the three TFNGs, and she'd grown close to Steve through her friendship with Sally.

The STS-41-D team quickly established itself as a rowdy bunch. Eventually they earned the nickname Zoo

Crew, and they lived up to it, always playing pranks and cracking jokes. Judy's crewmates repeatedly teased her about her big crush on the actor Tom Selleck, whose picture she pinned to the walls of her workplace.

But Judy never got seriously mad about teasing. Easygoing acceptance was her way of not making a big deal of her gender. Above all, Judy didn't want people to think that she'd gotten her position because of a trait of birth that was out of her control. She felt that she'd worked unbelievably hard to get there. "I think I'm where I am because I just happened to make the right decisions at the times when the decisions were presented to me," she told a reporter once. When asked if she credited the women's movement with her success, Judy said she didn't credit anyone.

Whether she wanted to or not, though, Judy was making history.

She would be the first Jewish American in space. It was another "first" the press clamored to ask her about, but Judy didn't highlight it any more than she did her gender. She didn't like being labeled. She once told her father, "Dad, I don't want to be a Jewish astronaut. I don't want to be a Jewish woman astronaut. I just want to be an astronaut, period. I just want to go out in space and do my job."

Her job was her prime focus. She'd thrown herself into her work, but her mission changed in the months before flight. "Don't fall in love with your payload" was a common saying in the Astronaut Office. No matter what your shuttle was tasked with carrying to space, it could change before you got off the ground.

Judy's flight was originally going to launch a massive communications satellite, but a problem with that satellite delayed its launch. The crew worried that their mission might be canceled, but instead they were given two smaller satellites.

Judy also got a new assignment all her own: unfurling a long rectangular solar panel. Using controls in the shuttle's cockpit, she'd roll the panel from inside the cargo bay out into space, where it was supposed to straighten and stiffen like a board. NASA wanted to see if this long solar panel could hold up in the extreme environment of space. If so, it could someday help future spacecraft collect solar power.

As an electrical engineer, Judy was the perfect person for the assignment. She'd also need to keep her robotic arm skills sharp. If the solar panel got stuck in space, Judy would use the arm to tuck it back into the shuttle.

Things changed again when a fifth member was assigned to the crew. Technically Charlie Walker wasn't even an astronaut. He worked for a private contractor and would be the first payload specialist, a non-astronaut who was connected to cargo or to an experiment, to fly in the space shuttle.

Charlie would travel to space with Judy in the mid-deck, the room beneath the cockpit that had just one small window and practically no view of the outside world. Judy and Mike Mullane had flipped a coin, and he'd won. He'd be one of the four crew members on the top level, with great views of the action on the ascent into space, while Judy would stare at a row of lockers—although she and Mike would swap seats for the return.

On June 25, 1984, Judy woke early, thrilled by the feeling that she'd be an astronaut at last. Just as Sally had done, Judy went through each pre-launch step before strapping into her seat. And with each step the tension heightened. Then, at T-minus thirty-two minutes, flight controllers told the crew there was a problem with the backup flight computer. At T-minus nine minutes the countdown entered a planned hold, with the clock stopped. But the computer issue couldn't be fixed in time to resume the countdown.

"*Discovery*, we're going to have to pull you out and try again tomorrow," a flight controller said over the intercom.

And the following day, Judy went through it all again. This time, at T-minus thirty seconds, Hank said to the crew, "Well, gang, we're going to go now unless something really bad happens." The backup computer was working just fine. It finally felt as if space was within their grasp.

Judy turned to Charlie lying next to her. Both their visors were closed by that point, hiding their faces. They reached toward each other and gripped hands for some last-minute solidarity. At that moment Judy was glad to have Charlie with her in the mid-deck.

"We have a go for main engine start," the announcer said on NASA TV. "Seven. Six. Five. We have main engine start."

A deafening blast sounded. The engines ignited at the shuttle's base, and *Discovery* started to tremble violently, sending vibrations through Judy's entire body. Judy braced herself for the lurch off the launchpad. She'd been waiting for that moment for years.

But just a second after the shaking had started, the movement suddenly ceased. A dreadful mechanical wrenching sounded throughout the cabin. The roaring engines fell silent. An eerie stillness filled the air—and the shuttle's master alarm started wailing like a police siren throughout the vehicle. *Discovery* sat on its launchpad, motionless.

That . . . wasn't supposed to happen.

"We have a cutoff, and we have an abort by the onboard computers of the orbiter *Discovery*," the announcer said to the public over the loudspeakers.

Everyone on the launchpad stayed absolutely silent, save for the seagulls screaming outside. Judy's mind raced. Shuttle engines had never before shut off an instant after igniting on the launchpad.

If the shuttle was unstable or dangerous in any way,

the astronauts might need to make a break for it. And it was her responsibility to open the hatch door to let everyone out. She'd practiced it during training, but she hadn't thought she'd ever have to do it. Her heart thumped as she tried to remember which knob to turn on the hatch door, and how fast she could get the thing open.

No one gave her the green light to open the door, though.

Everyone stayed ghostly quiet—fairly abnormal for the Zoo Crew. Right away Launch Control declared that the computers had picked up some unusual readings and then shut down the main engines before the solid rocket boosters—which were unstoppable once they ignited—could light up. Judy and the rest of the crew knew that if those boosters did ignite now, it would mean instant death.

Suddenly Mission Control began to panic. Their data showed that one of the three engines was still on. The crew knew that couldn't be right. The space shuttle was just sitting there. They later learned that a blocked valve in one of the engines had prevented it from starting—so it couldn't enter shutdown mode. And that made Mission Control think the engine was still running.

In the confusion the tension in the cabin grew thick. No one spoke unless they were responding to personnel on the ground. Everyone had questions, but they didn't want to interrupt the teams frantically working on the issue.

Judy just listened, waiting for instructions and hoping that everything would be okay. No one knew what to expect.

Then came the word no one wanted to hear: "fire." Just hearing it sent chills through everyone inside *Discovery*. A blaze near a rocket loaded with more than five hundred thousand gallons of extremely combustible fuel was a scary recipe for explosion. But flames had been detected on the side of the vehicle. Valves around the shuttle burst open, spraying thousands of gallons of water.

Hank told everyone to unstrap and get ready to move. If they bailed out, they'd have to speed across the catwalk to the launch tower. A series of metal baskets would take them to the ground quickly on cables—the world's most intense and scariest zip line. The crew waited for directions.

Finally, Judy couldn't take it. She made her way over to the hatch and peered out the window. Water ran down the side of the shuttle like torrential rain. The suspended walkway had snapped into position, an escape route to the baskets. But Judy couldn't see any fire.

"Do you want me to open the hatch?" she asked Hank.

They all debated whether it was wiser to stay seated or to make their grand escape. The last place they wanted to be was inside the shuttle if the fire reached the external fuel tank. Eventually Hank told Judy no. They were going to wait it out.

About forty minutes after the abort, flight personnel

arrived to open the hatch and help the crew out safely. Judy came out first, smiling. As the astronauts crossed the catwalk, water dripped onto them, soaking their flight suits. They were spared the basket ride to the ground, but there was an inch of water on the elevator floor.

The six drenched crew members shivered as they rode back to their quarters. Judy looked out the windows of the vehicle, watching *Discovery* grow tinier and tinier. She was completely miserable. Not only was she still on solid ground but she was now wet and freezing. "This is *not* how I thought spaceflight would be," Mike Mullane vented.

Judy couldn't have agreed more.

Once they'd dried off, the astronauts learned that the engines' brief ignition had created a bright flash and a large cloud of exhaust that had engulfed the shuttle. Spectators had expected the shuttle to climb into the sky, and when it hadn't, they'd feared the worst. The crew's families had had a brief moment of terror, thinking they were watching their loved ones die.

And had the crew decided to evacuate, that might have been the case. The fire NASA had detected on the launchpad wasn't your average fire. It was a hydrogen fire, fueled by the same bad valve that had aborted the launch. Hydrogen fires can burn clear, making them invisible to the naked eye. It's possible that if the crew had evacuated the shuttle when Judy had crawled out of her seat, they

186 • THE SIX

would have run headfirst into flames they couldn't see. The choice to stay inside may have saved their lives.

After the abort a reporter asked Judy how she felt. She put the best possible face on the situation. "I was disappointed. But I was relieved that the safety systems do work. It was unfortunate that we had to check them out. But it built confidence in the whole system."

For days the Zoo Crew feared the absolute worst. If their flight were canceled, they'd have to wait for another assignment. It might be months or even years down the line. But a couple of weeks later they learned that their flight was still on. And now they would have a third satellite to launch, as well as some additional experiments to do.

They waited one more month while *Discovery* got a new engine and engineers packed their new payloads. On August 30 they were back at the Cape, sitting inside the shuttle's cockpit once again. As they entered the T-minus-nine-minute hold, the entire crew groaned when flight control told them that someone in a private plane was flying too close to the pad, potentially triggering an abort.

Judy swore under her breath at the pilot's stupidity. Ultimately he was shooed out of the launch zone. The countdown continued.

And then . . . liftoff. After two failed launch attempts, Judy was finally on her way to space.

For the first two minutes it felt like a never-ending earthquake. Then the solid rocket boosters broke away and the surreal smoothness of flight began. *Discovery* entered orbit. Judy unstrapped from her seat to check on Charlie, who was suffering from a bout of Space Adaptation Syndrome.

When Mike Mullane came down from the top deck, he and Judy tumbled through the air together. They were celebrating their arrival in space—and the fact that they weren't spacesick like Charlie.

Immediately after the brief celebration, though, the STS-41-D crew were off to work, launching the first satellite. It sailed out of the cargo hold as expected. The next day, however, the launch of the second satellite ran into a snag.

It happened as the crew tried to film the launch with a massive IMAX camera. The footage was to be used in *The Dream Is Alive,* a documentary on the space shuttle. Judy floated next to Hank as he mounted the camera on his shoulders. With the lens pointed out the window, he captured the satellite floating out into the void.

Judy leaned in close. Suddenly she felt an intense, painful tugging on her scalp. She shrieked at the top of her lungs. A good chunk of her free-flying hair had been snagged in the drive belt of the IMAX camera. The men tried to help her pull out her hair, but the belt continued to munch as Judy screamed in agony. Finally enough hair had entered the camera to jam it to a halt.

Someone grabbed a pair of scissors to cut the captive hair free. Judy was okay, but now there was another problem. The camera, probably worth as much as one of the shuttle's parts, was too full of hair to work. It wasn't the end of the world, but it was still a failure that Mission Control needed to know about.

Just as Hank went to radio down to the flight controllers, Judy grabbed him. She insisted he not mention a single word about her hair jamming the camera. That went for the rest of the crew too. She begged them to take this secret to their graves.

It took a minute for them all to understand what Judy had realized at once. The press would go crazy with the story if it got out. No one would focus on the success of their mission. They'd all be talking about her and her hair. And because she was only the second American woman to fly in space, she still received intense attention. She might have worried that if the IMAX incident became public, people would debate whether women's hair should keep them from going into space.

With Judy's red-hot gaze burrowing into him, Hank explained to Mission Control that they'd been trying to capture the satellite as it moved away, and the camera "jammed." Mission Control didn't ask any follow-up questions. Eventually Mike Coats removed enough of Judy's hair to get the camera running again.

Unfortunately for Judy, even without the world knowing of the IMAX crisis, her hair became a main character on the flight. Video footage from the mission was making its way to Earth, showing the astronauts attending to their duties in space. At one point Judy scribbled "HI DAD" on a piece of paper and held it toward a camera. Marvin Resnik was surely thrilled to see the message, but the news anchors and the rest of the world didn't care. They were mostly focused on Judy's long, curly, raven-black hair. It fanned up and out in orbit, unlike Sally's shorter cut. With each turn of her head, her hair bounced. It followed her through the shuttle like a black halo.

Judy didn't realize how much of a splash these images were making until the morning when Mission Control woke the crew by playing the song "Hair" from the Broadway musical of that name. When it dawned on Judy that the world below was talking about her hair—the last thing she wanted to talk about—she let out a string of curses.

But then she went back to focusing on her tasks. Once the third satellite was launched, it was time for Judy to send out the hundred-and-two-foot-long solar panel. She radioed down to Mission Control that it had unfurled out of the payload bay as planned.

As the flight wound down, Steve noticed a weird

190 · THE SIX

reading on one of the computers. The temperature of an exit nozzle was far lower than it should have been. Whenever tanks on board became full of leftover water from the fuel cells, or urine, the liquid was dumped out through this nozzle, which was heated to make sure it didn't freeze in the cold of space. But the camera on the robotic arm revealed a chunky icicle of wastewater sticking out of the shuttle's side.

Engineers on the ground estimated that the icicle could weigh twenty-five to thirty pounds. Flight controllers worried that it could break off during reentry and damage the vehicle's side. There was talk of an unplanned space walk to remove the ice, which thrilled Mullane. But in the end the simplest solution was chosen. Hank used the robotic arm to knock off the ice.

Now Mission Control feared, though, that dumping more water out of the shuttle would create another icicle. The crew received an unwelcome command: don't urinate in the toilet anymore. They couldn't risk the tank getting too full. Mission Control reminded the crew that there were some old plastic urine bags on board—the same kind that had been used during the Apollo missions. The crew could use those.

But there was a twist. The CAPCOM on duty informed the crew that they had about "three man-days" left in the toilet tank. That meant that one person could use the toilet for the three days left in the mission. "And without saying it," Steve recalled later, "what he was really saying is, J.R. can use it."

Judy didn't go near the toilet. "Well, if you guys aren't going to use it, I'm not going to use it," she said. Once again Judy did not want to be singled out among her crewmates.

The result was, of course, a mess. In space, pee doesn't simply collect in a bag. When it hit the inside of the bag, it bounced, broke free, and floated about the cabin. The crew had to chase down and clean up the escaped droplets. Eventually they realized that stuffing socks into the bags would help soak up the pee, preventing it from escaping. One by one all the socks on board were sacrificed for the greater good of a urine-free cockpit.

Judy's decision not to use the toilet, it turned out, was a good one. After the shuttle landed, the wastewater tank was found to be completely full. If anyone had used the toilet, they'd probably have had to dump the tank again, risking another icicle.

After six days in space the crew returned to Earth, landing at Edwards Air Force Base. Judy was presented with a bouquet of roses. Remembering the fuss over Sally's, she held on to them.

A few days after the flight, the crew took part in the

usual press conference, sharing with the world what they'd experienced. Most of the questions were fairly standard, save for one.

"And one more quick question," a reporter asked over the phone. "For any women in the future who might be going up into space, any advice on hairstyles?"

Judy's response made it clear how she felt about that question. "No advice."

After the mission, NASA engineers and the agency's contractors did a full examination of *Discovery*, the solid rocket boosters, and what was recovered from the external tank. Engineers at the manufacturer of the boosters, the company whose name was now Morton Thiokol, saw something odd when they took them apart. They found a tiny bit of soot behind one of the primary O-rings, the thin rubberlike seals that kept the hot gases inside the booster from leaking out.

The soot showed that the O-ring had failed at its job. The gases had eaten away at the ring enough that the hot materials had broken through the seal for a short time. Fortunately, a secondary O-ring had prevented the gases from escaping into the open air.

Engineers had seen erosion of the O-rings before. In fact, other O-rings on STS-41-D had eroded. Never before, though, had they seen a breach, where the hot gases had blown completely through one of the seals. But engineers decided that this rare event was an "acceptable risk," and that shuttle flights could continue safely.

And the Six would continue to ride the shuttles to space. By the end of 1983, while Judy was training for her first mission, Kathy, Anna, Rhea, and Shannon had each been assigned to their own first flight. Their dreams were coming closer to reality.

CHAPTER SEVENTEEN

Kathy Walks into the Void

★ ★ ★ ★ ★ ★

Years before she flew in the space shuttle, Kathy made history by setting an unofficial world aviation record.

Early in her astronaut career Kathy had been assigned to train with the WB-57F, a jet that NASA used for researching Earth's atmosphere at high altitudes. Commercial jets usually fly between 31,000 feet and 42,000 feet—about six to eight miles—above the ground. The WB-57F could go much, much higher.

On July 1, 1979, Kathy and a pilot flew above west Texas. At their target height of 63,300 feet, almost twelve miles above the ground, the low air pressure could have made their blood start to boil. With the air force's helmeted pressure suits on, though, they had an uneventful research expedition. Kathy took images with an infrared camera and scanned the distant terrain in various wavelengths of light.

And she just happened to fly higher that day than any other woman ever had.

Kathy had been scared at first when she'd been assigned

to train with the WB-57F, but she wound up loving those high-flying planes on jaunts to Alaska, Peru, and points between. "That was very fun, other than this little bit of vague concern that, 'Hope this doesn't mean I'm falling off the face of the earth,'" Kathy said.

As she had hoped, Kathy became the first woman fully qualified to wear the air force pressure suit. She thought that her hundreds of hours spent in the suit were good preparation for wearing a space suit to walk outside the space shuttle one day. To help NASA agree with her, she volunteered to test space walk procedures.

Space walks were simulated in pools, to mimic the effects of weightlessness. There was just one drawback: the space shuttle suits weren't ready to use yet. Kathy had to wear Pete Conrad's old suit, as Anna had done. It had been too big for Anna, but it was about an inch too short for Kathy. It dug painfully into her shoulders, chest, and back. It took all her strength to walk over to the pool and flop into the tank. The pain instantly vanished in the weightless environment, but it made the point that space suits have to fit their wearers perfectly for a space walk to work.

Even so, Kathy loved simulated spacewalking so much that she did dozens of practice dives. But she wanted to wear a space suit in orbit, not in a pool, and she still had no idea when that day would come.

• • •

On the day of Sally's historic launch for the STS-7 mission, Kathy was in California getting ready for a different kind of dive: the final step in being certified as an open-water scuba diver. She watched the launch on television, even though a part of her wished it were her on board.

Six days later Kathy was back in Houston, listening to audio from STS-7 as the crew came in for a landing. When the weather at Cape Canaveral forced *Challenger* to plan a landing in California instead, NASA sent Kathy and astronaut P. J. Weitz to Florida to "entertain the VIPs"—the officials, media, celebrities, and others who had gathered there to greet Sally and her crewmates.

The second Kathy stepped into the auditorium at Cape Canaveral, a crowd of thousands descended on her, all buzzing with excitement. Kathy gulped, feeling completely unprepared to handle the swell of enthusiasm. Everyone wanted to see Sally.

At that moment Kathy was glad that Sally had landed in California. America's first woman astronaut would get a few precious hours alone with her crew before everyone in America—perhaps even the world—grabbed for a piece of her. "I was just instantly really happy for her that she had this little hiatus to make her own initial sense of the flight—to enjoy it and bask in the moment," Kathy said.

Then Kathy had another realization, one that had come to Judy as well: *If this is what you get for going first, she can have it!*

. . .

About a month later Kathy was on a long backpacking trip with friends through the Wind River Range in western Wyoming. With snowcapped peaks spread out before her, she finally stopped wondering when she would go to space. Then, during a break at a farm, she got a call.

Sally had some big news. Kathy was going to be assigned to her first spaceflight. The two of them would fly together on the mission, and Kathy would get to perform a space walk.

When she got back to Houston, Kathy got the official news from George Abbey, who asked if she wanted to do a real space walk. It was all Kathy had worked for over the last few years. Of course she happily accepted. Then she learned that when it came to spacewalking, NASA's medics wanted to treat her differently from the men.

One small study appeared to show that women were more likely than men to get "the bends," also called decompression sickness, which can occur when someone experiences a rapid drop in air or water pressure. With symptoms ranging from fatigue and muscle or joint pain to confused thinking, numbness, difficulty breathing, and chest pain, decompression sickness is potentially deadly. It can be a problem for scuba divers and those who fly at high altitudes. Because the air pressure inside space suits is somewhat lower than normal, all astronauts did a standard amount of "pre-breathing" of pure oxygen before putting on their suits. This flushed nitrogen from their bodies and made them less likely to get the bends. The medics, though, said that Kathy needed to do more pre-breathing than the men.

As a diver who'd never had any more trouble with the bends than her male colleagues, Kathy thought this was ridiculous. "I managed to keep my cool and not get drawn into feeling I was being accused personally of being unfit for spacewalking or that I was fighting a cosmic battle on behalf of all women," she said. As a scientist she knew that the right thing to do was take a hard look at the data.

And she found some big flaws. The researchers had studied only about fifty or sixty people—not a large sample size when it comes to statistics. They also hadn't accounted for other factors, such as body weight, that could contribute to the bends. Kathy pointed out these issues and got permission for the space walk with no special precautions.

Kathy's mission, STS-41-G, would be commanded by Bob Crippen, who'd been in charge of Sally's flight. He would be juggling two missions at the same time, flying them almost back-to-back, because NASA wanted to see just how quickly astronauts could move from one flight to another.

Bob was already training for 41-C, which would fly first. He'd told George that he'd fly 41-G as well, but only if he could have a crew member on the second whom he'd flown with before, someone who could help train the second crew while he was working with the first. He asked for Sally as that crew member, and so the first flight with two women was scheduled. Their TFNG classmate Jon McBride was 41-G's pilot, and Kathy's space walk partner was Dave Leestma.

Kathy and Dave had been working on an experiment to see if satellites could be refueled in space, somewhat like filling up a car's tank at the gas station. Refueling a spacecraft isn't easy, especially in orbit. Temperatures swing from blistering cold to scorching hot, depending on how the vehicle is exposed to the sun. On top of that, most satellites run on a nasty type of fuel called hydrazine. The putrid-smelling liquid is wildly toxic to humans. It also has a bad habit of exploding if it's heated enough and meets the right kind of spark.

Kathy and Dave had tested refueling approaches on the ground, and NASA now wanted them to see if it could be done in space during a space walk. They would perform the test in the shuttle's open cargo bay. Wearing space suits, they'd connect tanks so that hydrazine could transfer between the tanks. If the demonstration worked, it might be possible to give satellites longer life by topping up their fuel.

Bob made Dave the space walk lead, although Kathy surpassed him in experience and leadership. Kathy thought it was "bad optics"—something that wouldn't look good to the outside. But Bob had made the decision because Kathy was going to be the lead on another experiment. STS-41-G would carry a special imaging radar to capture pictures of Earth from various angles in orbit. Kathy's knowledge of geology made her a perfect fit to oversee that project, which to Bob meant that Dave had to oversee the space walk.

Regardless of who was lead, Kathy and Dave were going to be spending a lot of time together in the giant dive tank at the Johnson Space Center's Weightless Environment Training Facility. Soon after their assignments, the two met in one of NASA's giant hangars to suit up for their first space walk dress rehearsal. But once they arrived, they looked around and realized there weren't separate rooms to change in.

Dave recalled, "I look across at Kathy and she looks across and sees me and she goes, 'Whoops, is this the wrong place?' And I go, 'This is the only one.'" The area was just one massive open room. And both astronauts needed to fully undress to get into their liquid cooling garments: bodysuits threaded with tubes that would run water all over their bodies. On space walks these garments prevent astronauts from overheating while stuffed inside their cramped space suits.

The two stood next to each other, holding their bodysuits. Then Kathy turned to Dave. "Dave, let me tell you how I feel about modesty at a moment like this. I have none."

"Fine," Dave said, a bit relieved.

As they began to slip off their clothing in front of a room full of technicians who'd come to help with the simulation, the techs ran to the door to give them some privacy. Kathy chuckled to herself as she watched them go.

That was just the beginning of a long training process. Kathy and Dave spent hours upon hours in the pool, rehearsing the steps of their space walk until the movements were practically imprinted on their brains. The space walk itself was only meant to last a few hours. But they wanted to make it perfect.

When the 41-G flight assignments were announced, all signs pointed to Kathy making spaceflight history. She'd be the first woman to leave her spaceship and walk in space. Sally would make history again too. She'd be the first woman to fly to space for a second time.

But when a NASA employee congratulated Kathy and Sally, Kathy knew better. "No, you have not been paying attention," she said. "It's a very long time between today and that flight date. Let me just promise you a Soviet woman will fly a second flight and get a space walk." Kathy *had* been paying attention. She knew that the Soviets did whatever they could to reach space milestones first.

Sure enough, just months before the scheduled launch of 41-G, cosmonaut Svetlana Savitskaya launched into

202 • THE SIX

space for the second time. She docked with the Soviets' small Salyut 7 space station. While she was on board, Svetlana donned a space suit and exited the space station. For three hours and thirty-five minutes, she cut and welded metals in orbit with her male crewmate. Svetlana's flight took the title Sally had been in line for. Her space walk took Kathy's.

Back on Earth, NASA fumed, but Kathy took it in stride. She had suspected all along that it would happen. "First *American* woman to do a space walk" was a perfectly admirable title. Still, NASA tried to figure out a way to make it better. If Kathy just stayed out in space a few minutes longer than Svetlana, she'd set the record for longest space walk by a woman.

The idea amused Kathy. She and Dave had trained to hit their timeline tightly. It felt wrong to go slower just to make a point. "It didn't strike me as a really big thing to beat her by a few minutes," Kathy said. "I'm certainly not going to go tromping around on dinner speeches or something saying, 'Well yes, but I have the duration record,' because it's all of the same order. It's just silly."

As the launch grew closer, though, the idea of titles and firsts fell away. There was simply too much work to do. And then, bright and early on launch morning, the astronauts climbed inside *Challenger*. Seated next to Sally in the cockpit, directly behind the commander and the pilot, Kathy found herself in orbit just eight and a half minutes after takeoff. She was relieved that no glitches had prevented the launch. But STS-41-G was just getting started.

Unlike Sally's first flight, her second one—and Kathy's first—seemed full of issues. Nothing was life-threatening, but the crew felt that they were constantly solving problems.

The problems began with the Earth-observing satellite the crew was supposed to release on day one. Sally and Dave used the robotic arm to snatch it out of the payload bay, but once it was out, its solar panels didn't unfurl as they were supposed to. Mission Control and the astronauts tried to troubleshoot, but nothing worked.

The satellite was still attached to the arm, so flight controllers asked the crew to turn the shuttle to put the satellite into the sun. Just then the shuttle lost radio contact with the ground. This happened often at that time, when there were far fewer communications satellites in orbit than there are today.

With the flight controllers unable to hear them, Sally suggested they shake the satellite with the robotic arm. Bob's response was that of a lenient parent: "Okay, but don't break anything."

Dave and Sally waved the satellite back and forth, more vigorously than the satellite operators might have liked. And just as the shuttle regained radio contact with the ground, the satellite's solar panels unfurled, and the crew released it into space.

It was then time for Kathy to work on her lead project: using the Earth-imaging radar. Though the space walk was at the top of Kathy's mind, the radar was the main reason for the mission. Kathy pressed the necessary buttons, and the radar antenna unfolded outward like a blossoming flower. But when the first "petal" of the antenna extended, it flapped like the wing of a wounded bird. Kathy's heart raced. This wasn't supposed to happen. And now the whole antenna was swiveling back and forth. Kathy couldn't think of anything to do except carry on with the operation. She commanded the other panel to open.

That seemed to be the answer. The antenna calmed down and stayed stable, and Kathy avoided a heart attack. Unfortunately, the crew's problems with antennas were far from over.

Another antenna—one used for sending large amounts of data to Earth—also started to swivel uncontrollably. Mission Control ordered the crew to cut power to the mechanism that controlled the antenna's movement. That job went to Sally. All it took was removing a cable . . . buried behind a maze of wires and a wall of storage lockers. Sally did it, but now the antenna was stuck in one position.

The imaging radar was collecting immense amounts of data that had to be sent down to Earth through a relay satellite. With the antenna stuck, Bob had to move the shuttle around periodically so that the antenna pointed at a satellite. When no communications link was available, Kathy and Dave recorded the data themselves to send as soon as they got a link. They had to constantly swap out the tapes on the high-speed recorders.

All of this severely cut into the amount of time the radar could make observations—and then, to make matters worse, one of the relay satellites went down for a day. To give the radar more time to collect data and beam it back to Earth, Mission Control rescheduled the space walk from day five to day eight.

Kathy silently worried that the space walk might not happen. Day eight was the day before reentry, usually kept free of space walks so that the astronauts could prepare for the intense ride home. She couldn't even begin to think of the despair she'd feel if the space walk were canceled, after the years of hard work she'd put in to get to this point.

When the day came, though, she and Dave suited up, did the standard pre-breathing, and got ready to leave the spacecraft. When Kathy heard that they were a go for the space walk, they were the "sweetest words" ever.

"Although you've choreographed all of this, you just feel the momentousness that this is now actually for real," she would later say. Encased in her human-shaped spaceship, she followed Dave out the air lock and into the vast open payload bay of *Challenger*. The suit that dragged her down on Earth now felt as light as a feather. "That is really great," she said moments later.

The two floating astronauts immediately got to work. They began connecting the two fuel tanks, while taking pictures of their progress. "I don't need to tell you how much fun this is, do I?" Kathy quipped.

"Not at all," Bob responded.

In the midst of the experiment, Bob radioed them to take a quick breather. For just a few moments of awe, Kathy gazed out at the magnificent, glowing Earth, separated from her by only her helmet. The sight was beyond words.

Then she dove back into the refueling experiment. She had a job to do, after all. For three hours, she and Dave did exactly what they'd rehearsed endlessly on Earth. It was like a floating ballet against the backdrop of a slowly spinning planet.

Before she went inside, Kathy had to deal with the faulty radar antenna that had plagued the crew since day one. Attached to a tether to keep her from drifting off, she grabbed the edge of the shuttle, then "walked" her hands to the antenna, on the opposite side of the payload bay, with her feet pointed up and away.

For this flight, as for Judy's, the crew had brought the IMAX camera on board, and Jon McBride asked Kathy to pause so he could get it into position to film her. She remained still, looking "down" at her hands clasped on the shuttle's side. She felt as though she were in a handstand—until she lowered her gaze slightly and saw Venezuela and the Caribbean Sea below her.

In that moment her perspective suddenly shifted. Recalling it later as a vivid present-tense memory, she'd say, "As soon as I move my eyes off my hands and look level and then down a little bit, I feel like I'm not doing a handstand any longer. Now I feel like I'm hanging from a tree limb."

Kathy stowed the troublesome antenna, she and Dave performed a few more antics in their space suits, and it was time to come inside. Their recorded time outside was three hours and twenty-nine minutes, six minutes less than Svetlana's time. When a reporter later asked if Kathy was disappointed, she replied that she didn't care about records. "I could have been the 50,000th or 100,000th woman or human being to do a space walk," she said. "In terms of the broad historical backdrop, it still would have been my first space walk."

Before they returned home, Kathy spent her spare moments simply watching the view. She stared at the terminator—the line between daylight and darkness that travels across the spinning planet's surface. Because it took shuttle astronauts only ninety minutes to orbit Earth, they got to see more than a dozen sunrises and sunsets every day.

But as Kathy looked down at the nighttime side, watching the twinkling lights of the world's cities and highways below, she thought, *Right down there in one of those little patches of light right now, there could be a little girl looking up at the sky and pointing upward and saying to her mother, "Look, Mommy, it's a satellite." And she's pointing at me.*

It reminded her of when she was a little girl, pointing out satellites in the sky to her parents. Now she *was* that satellite.

And perhaps that girl down on Earth could one day travel to space like Kathy had—or even farther.

CHAPTER EIGHTEEN

Anna to the Rescue

N o way," Anna said, not a doubt in her mind.

She was on the *Today Show* in February 1984. She was there to talk about a space shuttle mission that was happening at the moment. Shortly before her appearance the shuttle crew had released two huge communications satellites, one for the nation of Indonesia and the other for the Western Union company. The satellites had engines attached to them to boost them into their final orbits. Unfortunately, the engines of both satellites had failed, and they were stranded in space.

Under the white-hot lights of the television studio, Anna fielded question after question about the failures. Her "no way" was the answer to a question about whether NASA would try to retrieve those satellites, and she was confident when she said no.

The satellites were massive bus-sized cylinders covered in solar panels. You couldn't just pluck them out of space and bring them back home, as if you were fetching apples from an orchard. But Anna was wrong, as it turned out.

And the failure of those two satellites would be the best thing that could happen for her spaceflight career.

By that time Anna had had her first flight assignment for more than half a year. She'd gotten it right after serving as the lead astronaut support person at Cape Canaveral for Sally's historic flight. Working on that launch had been an incredible experience. She and Sally had gotten to test some of the payloads together at Cape Canaveral just before the mission had taken off. At the time Anna had been eight months pregnant. Photos of her working alongside Sally showed a large baby bump beneath her flight suit.

Two weeks before she was due to give birth, George Abbey summoned both the Fishers, Anna and Bill. He wanted to assign Anna to a future flight. And since she was about to give birth, he wanted to know if she or Bill had any reservations about it.

Anna beamed. She'd dreamed of going to space since that day in the schoolyard listening to Alan Shepard's launch. Of course she didn't have any reservations, she told George. And the fact that her boss had confidence that she'd be able to train for her flight with a newborn meant the world to her. She accepted without hesitation.

Anna's flight would eventually be numbered STS-51-A. With Rick Hauck as commander, Anna and three other astronauts would have a pretty straightforward mission. They'd launch a satellite with a different type of rocket attached to boost it into higher orbit. To Rick the flight was "plain vanilla."

Anna started prepping for her flight while waiting for the first sign of labor pains. A month later, after a full day of training at the Johnson Space Center, Anna finally went into labor. She and Bill welcomed their daughter, Kristin, the next morning. But Anna had spent a lot of her working life in medical environments. She didn't want to stay in the hospital long.

She felt strong, so she did something a little bold. Just three days after giving birth, she showed up at the all-astronauts meeting at JSC, surprising everyone. Her presence made a clear statement: *I'm here, and nothing's going to change.* "I didn't want anyone to think that just because I'd had a baby that I wasn't going to be able to do what I had committed to," Anna said.

Determined to prove her commitment to her job, Anna didn't take a formal maternity leave. Instead the training team created a schedule that gave her days off to be home with Kristin. It worked well for a while. But then Anna decided to take on another role that would require a lot of time and effort. She wanted to be a CAPCOM, a role that astronauts covet.

But it was a job that Anna's commander didn't want her to take. He feared it would distract from her training for their mission. Anna insisted that being a CAPCOM *was* training. She'd learn what Mission Control was like during a flight, and how to communicate from space with the flight controllers on the ground. She told Rick it would make her a better crew member, and he eventually agreed.

So for a time Anna juggled it all. She trained with her crew, took care of a newborn at home with Bill, and talked back and forth with astronauts in space. On top of all that, she was breastfeeding. And in the early 1980s, facilities for new mothers—or women in general—weren't a priority for NASA. Women working in Mission Control had to trek to the far side of the building for a restroom. Anna sneaked away there during her shifts to pump milk.

As Anna was adjusting to her new roles of mother and crewmate, she and her crew were also adjusting to an entirely new mission. Their expected payload changed to launching two new communications satellites. And they might do something else—something completely new. The two stranded satellites that Anna had said would never be recovered could be coming back in a big way.

The insurance companies that had insured those satellites had been forced to fork out $180 million to Indonesia and the Western Union. That put the insurance companies in charge of the cargo—and they wanted it back, so that they could try to repurpose the satellites to make up some of their losses. The companies urged NASA to form a rescue mission to bring the satellites home.

It was a lot to ask. The insurers wanted a type of human spaceflight mission that had never been done before. The satellites were racing around Earth at roughly 17,500 miles an hour. The space shuttle crew would have to chase them down and match their speed precisely in order to catch them rather than crash into them. Then the astronauts would have to pluck the satellites out of space and tuck them inside the shuttle's cargo bay for the trip home.

Only one space shuttle mission had ever tried something similar. During the STS-41-C mission, astronauts had caught up to a malfunctioning NASA satellite called Solar Max to grab and repair it. They'd succeeded, but they had been plagued with challenges. Scariest of all, a spacewalking crew member had almost been lost in space.

And Solar Max had been made to be caught. It had been built with a handle in case astronauts wanted to grab hold of it one day. The stranded satellites had no handles. They were mostly smooth and round. To grab on to them NASA would have to develop a piece of hardware that had never been made before.

Still, a few things convinced NASA that the mission could be accomplished. The success of the Solar Max job had boosted the agency's confidence. Also, NASA had a new Manned Maneuvering Unit (MMU)—a jet backpack that could move astronauts around on space walks without tethers attaching them to a shuttle. NASA pictured an astronaut strapping on the MMU, floating out from the shuttle, and somehow maneuvering the lost-in-space satellites back to the cargo bay.

Getting to try a completely new type of flight was an astronaut's dream. Anna and her crew just hoped the rescue mission would come to them. Fortunately, their commander, Rick Hauck, had shown off his skills on Sally's first mission, when he'd flown the shuttle close to the SPAS-01 satellite—the payload that Sally had used the robotic arm to grapple with. NASA figured Rick could oversee the same thing again, only with two big satellites.

Once the satellite retrieval mission became official, the training for STS-51-A went into overdrive. Anna's crew would carry out one of the most daring space walks ever. Dale and Joe, the spacewalkers, immersed themselves in NASA's training pool. Anna would have a critical job inside the shuttle. She'd use the robotic arm to help snag the satellites and lower them into the cargo bay. The three astronauts would pass the satellites to one another as the pilot and commander kept the space shuttle steady.

There was just one tiny problem. How were they supposed to grab these satellites? Dale sketched out the design for a device that became known as "the stinger." It looked like a giant spike. It would be jabbed inside the nozzle of the satellite's engine, and then the spacewalker holding the stinger could flip a handle to make the device expand. This would plug the engine and give them a way to hold on to the massive satellite. Joe once described it as "like opening an umbrella inside a chimney."

With less than half a year to prepare, the team had to come up with new tools and procedures that no other crew had used. Anna practically lived in the simulator with the robotic arm. Sometimes she brought Kristin with her for the late-night practice sessions.

Anna never had the same onslaught of media attention as Sally, but she was still much talked about. After all, she'd make history as the first mother in space. (Apparently the Soviet Union didn't have a female cosmonaut they could send up to steal that title.)

The press was fixated on Anna's motherhood. WHEN MOM IS AN ASTRONAUT, one headline declared. Plenty of fathers had already been to space, but that didn't seem to matter. Everyone wondered how a mom could possibly leave her child for a week to go to space. That said a lot about how the world of the 1980s still viewed a mother's place and her priorities.

For Anna it was simple. This was her job. "I had made up my mind what I was going to do, and I never wavered from that decision," she said. After Kristin was born, Anna received a letter from a "concerned" citizen who felt it important to tell Anna just how irresponsible she was being.

Bill tore the letter up. "Don't read these things," he told her. She decided to ignore anything negative that was written about her.

Instead of worrying about the critics, the Fishers leaned into the moment. They had a tiny NASA flight suit made for Kristin, who went with her mother to a round of interviews at NASA. Photographers snapped mother and daughter in the simulator's cockpit.

Anna's team began the standard weeklong quarantine on October 31, 1984, but Anna fudged the rules a little that first day. It was Kristin's first official Halloween, and Anna didn't want to miss it. Anna went trick-or-treating with Kristin and Bill to a few houses in their neighborhood. Fortunately for Anna, no one at NASA even noticed she was gone.

One thing Anna made sure to do before her flight was to write a letter to Kristin. "No matter what happens in the future . . . in spaceflight or in our relationship . . . she came along and gave me incredible joy, a balance and perspective that made me a better person," Anna said later of the letter's contents. She sealed it and planned to give it to her daughter when she was older—long after Anna had come back from space.

But Anna still hoped to see her daughter one last time before boarding her ride to orbit. Bill tried to make it happen by bringing Kristin and Anna's mother in a van close to where Anna was staying so they could watch her walk out on launch morning, although they had to stay hidden. Technically none of them was supposed to be on-site in this way. Bill warned Elfriede, Anna's mother, not to leave the van under any circumstances.

As Anna slowly walked toward the crew vehicle, she frantically scanned the crowd of onlookers to see if she could catch a glimpse of Kristin, but she couldn't spot her daughter. Her mother saw the distress in Anna's eyes, and that's when grandma went rogue. Elfriede opened the passenger door and emerged with Kristin hoisted high in her arms. The minor indiscretion paid off. Anna locked eyes on her daughter and felt immense relief. She'd seen Kristin. *Okay, that's behind me*, she thought. Now she could focus on the task at hand.

A little while later Anna and her crew climbed into the shuttle cockpit, strapped into their seats—and then learned that the launch was being scrubbed. Winds high above the site were rough.

Twenty-four hours later Anna repeated her movements, but this time she felt like the launch was actually going to happen. And once again Elfriede broke the rules to give Anna a last look at Kristin while Bill fumed inside the van.

Anna was the second-to-last person to climb into the shuttle. While the others strapped into their seats, she lingered for a few extra moments on the walkway that connected the launch tower to the cockpit. In those early-morning hours a full moon shone brilliantly white over the inky-dark Atlantic.

"I cannot tell you what it was like to stand there thinking

way back to that time when I was twelve years old, listening to Al Shepard launch, wondering if I would ever have a chance," Anna would later say. "And here I [was] standing and getting ready to launch into space. . . . It was such a surreal feeling."

As flight engineer Anna sat behind the pilot and the commander, like Sally on her first flight. This gave her an incredible view out the front windows. The view from the grounds of Cape Canaveral was impressive too. Kristin watched as the shuttle carrying her mother soared into the sky. She pointed up at the glowing dot inching above the horizon. "Oh no, Mama," she said. Once the spacecraft faded from view, Bill asked his daughter "where Mama was." She simply pointed up.

When the main engines cut off, Anna could feel the blood almost instantly rush to her face. On Earth, gravity makes the body's liquids pool down in the legs. In weightlessness the liquids shift upward, spreading evenly throughout the head and arms. Anna noticed in the mirror that the small wrinkles she'd spotted at home had miraculously disappeared.

But something else happened almost immediately. Anna felt sick. The dreaded Space Adaptation Syndrome had hit her. She resisted the urge to puke and the urge to take a nap, trying to stick to her assigned duties. She could still function, but she avoided all food for the first couple of days. She wondered why she'd pined for space. *I feel terrible,* she thought. *Why did I do this?*

Fortunately for Anna, the first few days featured the easier assignments. The crew released two satellites with no glitches. And on the third day, Anna had her own release—from sickness. It was as if someone flipped a switch inside her, making her nausea disappear. Rick could tell just by looking at her. "Anna is back with us," he said. That morning she ate a hot dog. It was the best she'd ever eaten, she said, on Earth or in orbit. Now she could start having the space experience she'd always dreamed about.

With the cargo bay emptied, the crew prepped to recover the two stranded satellites. On the fifth day, Anna sat next to Rick. Together they calculated all the tiny engine burns Rick would have to perform at just the right moments to catch up with the first satellite, called Palapa B2. While Joe and Dale put on their space suits, Rick crept up on the satellite. With every burn of the shuttle's thrusters, Rick and Anna triple-checked each other's calculations. At fifty miles out Rick could see the satellite in a navigational instrument. It looked like a tiny star. That "star" grew bigger and brighter until the cylinder was slowly rotating in front of them.

Rick parked *Discovery* just thirty-five feet from Palapa—a mere hair's breadth in the expanse of their orbit around Earth. This would give the spacewalkers the shortest possible distance to travel. With only so much gas in their jet packs, they had just seven hours to wrangle each spacecraft and stow it in the cargo bay. Rick kept *Discovery* steady while the spacewalkers emerged from the air lock.

Dale monitored the operation from inside the open payload bay while Joe used his jet pack to move forward inch by inch, holding the stinger. From inside the shuttle Anna and the others watched. Joe looked a bit like a white knight taking part in the world's most sluggish joust.

Once Joe had reached the satellite's back side, Joe stabbed the stinger inside the engine nozzle and expanded it. With his cargo on a stick, Joe, the smallest man in the astronaut corps, now looked like the world's strongest man as he slowly swung the twelve-hundred-pound Palapa around, positioning it for Anna. She guided the robotic arm up to the stinger, latched on to it, and took Joe for a ride. Still holding on to Palapa, he sailed up and over the shuttle as Anna dragged them to the payload bay, where Dale was waiting.

Joe was meant to attach a clamp to help the robotic arm guide the satellite into the payload bay, but when the clamp didn't fit, he guided Palapa in using just his hands. He stood with his feet anchored to the payload bay, holding the massive satellite while Dale removed the stinger and prepared the satellite to fit snugly inside the bay. For a good ninety minutes Joe stood with arms outstretched, holding the satellite still even when muscle cramps kicked in. Finally Dale and Joe used their arms to slide the satellite into the bay, like a key into a lock.

They did the same thing with the second stranded satellite, Westar 6, the next day. This time Dale got to wear the jet pack and stab the satellite with the stinger. The spacewalking duo posed for a photograph with their catch neatly tucked into the shuttle cargo hold, jokingly holding a FOR SALE sign written in bright red letters.

President Ronald Reagan called the astronauts while they were still in space to congratulate them on a job well done. He asked Anna if she'd recommend the career of astronaut to her daughter.

"Oh, that I would, Mr. President," Anna replied. "The experience is just everything I expected and even more. Seeing the world below us, it makes you realize just how we're all just part of this world. It's a truly incredible experience, and I'm going to recommend it to her highly."

Reporters on the ground also got some minutes with the crew in space. One European reporter asked Anna if she thought being an astronaut was "compatible with a mother's affection and task."

Anna laughed and said that she did think so. "I very much enjoy being a mother; it's a wonderful experience," she replied. "The space program is something that I also believe a great deal in, and I think as we've demonstrated on this flight, there's a tremendous capability there. I don't think the two are incompatible. I think that it's important for me as a person to do the things I believe in, and I think Kristin will benefit from that. Certainly, she'll have a lot of new bedtime stories."

Anna's answer was polite, but she hoped it had shown the foolishness of the question, which carried the weight of sexism. No one asked the men, most of whom had children, if their job was compatible with fatherhood.

After the crew landed, the world's opinions of Anna's flight continued to trickle in. One woman wrote a letter to the editor of the *Philadelphia Inquirer*, commenting that a picture of Anna in space next to a photo of her daughter graphically illustrated "the problems of today's society." The writer said, "To me, Anna Fisher is not a heroine, but a woman who is derelict in her duty."

Others didn't see it that way. Five months later the National Mother's Day Committee informed Anna that she'd be receiving the Mother of the Year award. (Six other women, including a daytime soap opera star and the governor of Kentucky, also received it.)

Anna found it ironic that she'd earned this award by leaving her daughter for a week. But she enjoyed the bragging rights that came with it. Later, when Kristin was grown and understood the tremendous milestone that Anna had achieved, she playfully pointed out that her mother owed everything to her.

CHAPTER NINETEEN
Rhea and the Space Heist

Rhea gathered with other astronauts in front of a television in June 1984. They were taking a break from work to watch the launch of the brand-new shuttle *Discovery*, with Judy in its crew. The room quieted as everyone listened to the countdown. At T-minus six seconds *Discovery*'s engines ignited—and then immediately shut off.

Rhea and the others leapt to their feet. Some yelled for the astronauts to get out of the cockpit. Others barked back that they should stay where they were. No one knew the right call, because they'd never seen an engine abort like this.

They all breathed a sigh of relief when their fellow astronauts eventually left the cockpit. Then they began to wonder what this meant for the shuttle flight lineup. Rhea was particularly eager to know—after this flight, hers was supposed to be next.

She'd been called to George Abbey's office a month after Sally's historic flight. A small part of her had wondered if it might be a mission assignment, but she'd doubted it. As the mother of a toddler, she was no longer going to the weekly get-togethers where people socialized with George. When not working at NASA, she was chasing her son, Paul, through the house or trying to keep her medical expertise sharp by working weekends at a hospital emergency room. Sometimes she wondered if she was really giving NASA the best version of herself.

But George surprised her. "Okay. I was wondering if you'd like to fly on STS-41-E next year?"

"Yes, sir!" Rhea accepted jubilantly. She would fly in mid-1984, the third woman in space, right after Judy. And she'd be the first mother in space. But what really mattered was that she'd finally get to fly—the one goal of every astronaut. The assignment felt extra sweet because many of her TFNG classmates hadn't received their calls yet.

Soon she was thrust into a whirlwind of mission training, ER practice, and motherhood. During normal working hours she was all NASA. Her commander was Karol "Bo" Bobko, who'd flown on the mission just before Sally's flight. Her other crewmates were Dave Griggs, Don Williams, and Jeff Hoffman. Rhea hadn't been particularly close with any of them, but she liked them and got along with them during training. Their mission would involve releasing a satellite and later retrieving it and placing it back into the bay. Rhea was put in charge of the robotic arm for this task, one of the most complicated parts of the mission.

Just when Rhea thought the stress couldn't get more overwhelming, George asked if she wanted a second assignment, for a flight in 1986. Rhea couldn't say no. The main payload for this mission would be a module called Spacelab, a laboratory designed to fit inside the shuttle's payload bay, where astronauts could do experiments in space. For one of the few doctor astronauts at NASA, it was a dream assignment.

For months Rhea tried her best to juggle the two missions, feeling entirely overwhelmed. Then Judy's aborted flight changed everything. George and other NASA officials did some quick musical chairs with the shuttle flights and crews. They rearranged things so that certain payloads got to space on time. And Rhea's scheduled first flight was simply taken off the schedule.

Rhea couldn't believe it. Space had been less than two months away. Now she couldn't say for sure if she'd ever fly. The uncertainty was infuriating. "I called my father and ranted," Rhea would later write. "I raged to Hoot until he got tired of listening. I thought about getting in my car and abandoning the whole place."

Hoot tried his best to encourage her, but it was hard to find the bright side. "She was pretty miserable. She felt like her whole crew was just the total down-and-out crew," Hoot said. "And I can't blame her."

The next month, NASA decided that Rhea's crew would take up another satellite . . . in March 1985. For Rhea it almost felt like moving to the back of the line.

As she trained for the new mission, she watched other women in her class make the history-making flights she was supposed to have made. Kathy became the third American woman in space, with an impressive space walk as a bonus. Anna became the first mother in space, with her daughter stealing the media show.

"In the grand scheme of life perhaps these weren't major losses, but they were important to me," wrote Rhea. But when Rhea later told a friend how the lineup change had disappointed her, the friend replied, "Who ever remembers any of that?"

It was a direct but fair point. Of course history would remember Sally Ride as the first American woman to fly. Beyond that, which of the Six did what would be quickly forgotten by most.

Although Rhea's flight had been restored to the lineup, it had changed. The payloads that the crew had trained on for a year disappeared. Now they were working with a new type of satellite, one so massive that it filled the payload bay. There wouldn't be any room for a robotic arm for Rhea to tinker with.

The crew grew larger too. A French payload specialist named Patrick Baudry would bring medical experiments to space, which interested Rhea. The other new crew member wasn't a specialist, though.

Jake Garn, a Republican senator from Utah, would be the first politician to fly to space.

Garn had raised the possibility back in 1981, just after the first shuttle had taken to the skies. Because Garn was a pilot—and especially because his Senate committee oversaw NASA's budget—the agency eventually decided to take him up. After all, the shuttle was meant to be a reliable truck that could take anyone into space. Why not a senator?

Most of the astronauts silently hoped the senator wouldn't end up in their crew. They'd already had to accept payload specialists who weren't astronauts. They didn't want the responsibility of having to babysit a lawmaker who basically had nothing to do. But Rhea was more positive. Their flight was going to be pretty ordinary. Perhaps a gimmick like taking a senator to space would add some sparkle to their mission.

Then, a little more than a week before the scheduled launch of Rhea's flight, fate stepped in again. Engineers found a defect in the booster on the satellite they were supposed to fly. It went back to the factory. Again Rhea worried that her flight might get dropped from the schedule. She said, "We felt like the most snake-bit crew that had ever existed."

But this time George Abbey told them that their flight was still on. They'd be getting a different payload, though— the same two types of communications satellites they had originally been supposed to launch. Patrick Baudry was bumped to a later flight, but payload specialist Charlie Walker was added because his experiment had already been installed on *Discovery*, the shuttle that Rhea's crew would now use. Senator Garn asked to fly with the original crew he'd trained with, so he remained on Rhea's flight.

The robotic arm was back in the payload bay too, but a different piece of cargo caught Rhea's eye: an echo-cardiogram machine, which uses ultrasound to observe the human heart. Medical professionals wanted to see whether the movement of body fluids in space made the heart change shape. As the doctor on the flight, Rhea took great interest in this experiment. She set about recruiting her crewmates as test subjects.

Quarantine began a week ahead of launch, in April 1985. Rhea missed Paul and felt guilty being separated from him. They could talk on the phone, but at just under three years old, Paul wasn't a master of phone conversation. Rhea needed to be near him one more time before she took flight—in case the unthinkable occurred.

One day during quarantine Rhea made a stealthy trip to her home just a couple of miles away. She sat with Paul in his playroom for a few minutes before grabbing his face in her hands. Looking into his eyes, she told him she loved him and asked him to remember her face until she came home. As if Paul could sense her anxiety, he gave her a big hug and planted a kiss on her cheek. Rhea tearfully left the house to return to quarantine. No one knew about her secret trip before the flight.

After "four different crew pictures, four different crew patches, three different payloads, and two different orbiters," as Rhea would later write, when launch day came, *Discovery*'s liftoff was problem-free. Once Rhea finally got to space, she even felt that STS-51-D was turning out to be a pretty boring mission. In spaceflight, though, boring is often good.

Some on board, including the senator, had serious bouts of Space Adaptation Syndrome. Not Rhea. She didn't feel a bit of nausea and was focused on her tasks.

On the first day, Dave and Jeff released a communications satellite for Canada. Rhea worked with the robotic arm to get a good look at the satellite's planned thruster firing, which went flawlessly. The crew felt proud.

Next Rhea got her hands on the echocardiogram machine. She used the equipment on herself and then roped in Jeff, Charlie, and Senator Garn as subjects. It took some persuading to move the senator across the cabin to the machine.

On day two it was time to release the second satellite. Rhea flipped all the necessary switches and pushed all the right buttons to set it up. Jeff, the lead on the release, double-checked her work and gave her a thumbs-up. Then she hit the button to set the satellite loose into the void. Through the cockpit window they saw the giant cylinder glide from inside the payload bay and inch out into space.

Soon the Syncom IV-3 satellite would extend its upper antenna to start communicating with the ground below. Then it would put itself into a spin and move away from the shuttle for about forty-five minutes. The satellite would travel halfway around the world before its boosters fired to send it to its higher, final orbit.

But after a little over a minute, Jeff noticed that the Syncom's antenna hadn't extended.

Everyone turned and peered out the windows. Jeff was right. The antenna was still in the off position. And the satellite wasn't starting to spin faster.

Rhea broke the news to Mission Control. She knew her words were probably causing a slight state of panic. A malfunctioning satellite was the last thing anyone wanted to deal with, but the Syncom IV-3 looked dead in space.

Flight controllers in Houston told the commander, Bo, to perform a short burn of the engines to trail close behind the satellite.

Uh, what? Rhea and the others were all immediately

curious. But NASA didn't clue them in on any concrete plans, and they all went to bed that night feeling a little dejected.

Rhea knew that the failure was no fault of theirs. The crew's job was simply to deploy the satellite, which they had done. The stuck antenna and the failed thruster were problems for the satellite's maker. Still, it was hard not to feel disappointed. To have just 50 percent of the cargo working felt like a screwup.

The next morning NASA gave the crew a startling wake-up call.

NASA had a plan to save the satellite. It sounded like an elaborate heist operation. Bo would maneuver the shuttle close to the Syncom, as Anna and her crew had done when they'd plucked the dead satellites Palapa and Westar out of space. But Rhea's crew would then do something completely new. Engineers thought the failure might have been caused by a switch on the outside of the satellite that had gotten stuck in the off position. The astronauts might be able to reach it.

NASA's first idea had been to simply send Jeff out into space to flip the switch. "I was going to go out and hold on to the end of the robotic arm with one hand and flick the switch on the satellite with my other," Jeff said years later. "But they decided that was a little bit too sporty." The new plan was for two astronauts to do a completely unplanned space walk to fit some kind of device to the end of the robotic arm. Then one of the astronauts on board the shuttle would maneuver the arm and use the device to flip the switch.

Rendezvousing with another object in space is no easy task. The crew had barely trained for it, because they hadn't been expecting to do it. As for flipping a switch with the robotic arm, how could they have trained for something like that? No one had tried anything like it in the history of the space program.

But Jeff and Dave lit up at the thought of doing a space walk. On Earth they'd trained for an emergency space walk, though they'd never thought it would happen. And Rhea would get one of the most important jobs. She'd operate the robotic arm and use it to flip the stuck switch on the satellite's surface. Turning the Syncom back on would depend on her skilled hand-eye coordination.

Suddenly this launch wasn't so boring after all. The crew agreed to the heist and dove into their appointed tasks.

First they had to craft the makeshift device that had been designed to be attached to the end of the arm. This turned out to be a major headache. Although the crew could send images to flight controllers on the ground, the controllers had no way to send pictures to the shuttle, just text. So the ground crew described what they wanted over the radio and sent instructions to the printer on the shuttle—including illustrations made of hundreds of spaced-out *X*s.

Rhea, Jeff, and Dave got to work on space arts and crafts. Rhea used a bone saw from the emergency medical kit to saw off parts of an aluminum tube from a circuit breaker. These became handles for the two devices NASA wanted the astronauts to make. The crew sacrificed plastic covers from their checklists to make other pieces. These were wrapped in duct tape. To help everything stay together in the vacuum of space, Rhea and Jake Garn stitched some of the parts together with needle and thread from the space suit repair kit. As Rhea plunged a needle through duct tape and plastic, she recalled stitching up abdomens in the emergency room.

The result was two makeshift plastic paddles with large rectangular cutout holes. The crew called them the fly-swatter and the lacrosse stick. The idea was that both could be used to catch hold of the switch on the outside of the satellite, and at least one of them would have enough force to move it. Rhea showed off the finished work to Mission Control, which marveled at how well the crew had followed the instructions.

Taping and stitching was just the first step. To help the crew get ready for a never-before-done maneuver, NASA sent a massive checklist of all the procedures ahead. About thirty feet of yellow paper spilled out of the printer. It filled almost every inch of open space in the cockpit. The crew carefully collected it, cut the rolls into pages, and taped them over a checklist they had already used. Now they had a binder for the upcoming operation.

On day five Jeff and Dave jubilantly wriggled into their space suits. They took the flyswatter and lacrosse stick outside to strap them to the robotic arm. The sun was setting behind Earth, bathing the open bay in deep red light.

Rhea and the others watched through the windows, unable to believe it was happening. An unplanned space walk was a first in shuttle history. The spacewalkers had no foot restraints or special tools, only tethers to tie themselves to the shuttle. They walked on their hands to the end of the robotic arm, which Rhea had positioned near the payload bay. In microgravity such a task isn't as simple as it might seem. Even a mistaken turn of a wrist can send a spacewalker twirling in the wrong direction.

It took Jeff and Dave about an hour to attach the two implements: the flyswatter and the lacrosse stick. Afterward NASA wanted to make sure that the robotic arm would still fit into the payload bay with its new attachments. Otherwise they'd have to do a second space walk to remove the devices. But the sun was setting again, and the light wasn't great for Rhea to test the arm's fit. Mission Control asked Dave and Jeff if they could stay outside for another forty minutes to wait for sunrise.

"Well, I'm sure you know how tough that's going to be," Jeff replied, elated.

Rhea watched as they crawled all around the payload bay, relishing every minute of extra playtime. They even crawled to the cockpit windows to get their picture taken. "So there I was out in a space suit, just watching the world go by with nothing to do," Jeff said.

With the sun shining on the orbiter again, Rhea demonstrated that the arm fit just fine in the bay with the flyswatter and lacrosse stick attached. The spacewalkers returned to the cabin with the widest of grins on their faces. All the crew felt it: this space heist might actually work.

On rendezvous day everyone wondered if Bo and Don could maneuver the shuttle close enough to the Syncom satellite without ramming it. They'd barely trained for such a move. Rhea also felt pressure. It was her job to use the arm to tug the Syncom's switch. If all went well, the lever would tear through the plastic devices but the force would pull the switch into the right position.

Bo and Don began to maneuver the shuttle closer to the Syncom. Bigger and bigger the satellite became, until it loomed large in the field of view, a massive cylinder with its booster pointed straight at the shuttle. "Somehow this was the moment that I started taking this operation seriously," Rhea would later write. She knew that if that booster ignited, they were toast. The entire crew banked on the satellite staying calm during their operation.

The timing had to be precise. If the switch was flipped at the right time, the Syncom would burn its thrusters forty-five minutes later—part of its original plan. NASA wanted to be sure the satellite was in the right spot in space when that burn took place. Rhea had a window of only a few minutes to snag and flip the switch.

As she waited, she pinpointed the target switch on the satellite. Using the robotic arm's camera, she took a picture of it. The sight was a little disheartening—the switch looked like it was already in the on position. Still, maybe an extra tug was all the satellite needed.

With a flick of the wrist and a turn of the knob, Rhea slowly put the arm into position, its two makeshift devices outstretched. The Syncom IV-3 was spinning, and she had to pull on the lever just as it rotated into the right position.

The moment came, Rhea inched the arm forward, and . . . success! The flyswatter caught on the switch, which tore through the plastic. In case that hadn't been enough, they waited for the satellite to do one full turn and snagged the lever again, this time with the lacrosse stick. The Syncom came around again for one last try. "We got, as we can count, at least three really good whacks at it," Rhea said after the mission.

Rhea had done it. She'd completed the space heist! She and her crew had carried out NASA's instructions flawlessly.

Unfortunately, the astronauts' actions didn't revive the

satellite. Whatever was wrong was inside it, and there was nothing the astronauts could do. This time Rhea and her crewmates were proud anyway. They might not have saved the satellite, but they'd completed a complicated mission never before performed. Their reward was an extra day in orbit, which they spent playing with toys like Slinkies and yo-yos, a fun experiment to show kids how these objects behaved in weightlessness.

Once the crew had landed back on Earth, Rhea learned that her flight had gotten a lot of press coverage after all—not just because of Senator Jake Garn but because of their unplanned salvage effort. Anna later told Rhea that a couple of the astronauts who considered themselves experts on the robotic arm had doubted Rhea's ability to pull off the stunt. Rhea never said an angry word to them. Success, she felt, was the greatest form of revenge.

But an ally at NASA had stuck up for her during the flight. As Rhea had stitched together the lacrosse stick and flyswatter, someone in Mission Control had commented that she was "a good seamstress"—a term used for women who sew. Sally Ride happened to overhear the remark. She tapped the person on the shoulder and corrected them.

"Good *surgeon*," Sally said.

CHAPTER TWENTY

Shannon Flies with a Prince

★ ★ ★ ★ ★ ★

After years of waiting without one complaint, it was Shannon's turn at last.

Shannon wasn't one to seek the spotlight. She didn't get caught up in the politics of jockeying for an early flight assignment. Shannon had joined NASA as a working mother of three. That meant skipping after-work social events. When the other women got together to discuss concerns related to their group, she'd usually miss that, too. "After hours, I couldn't do much," Shannon recalled. "I mean, I was home. I didn't have a whole lot of outside time to do social things."

But she kept her head down and worked hard at whatever job she was given, hoping it would lead to an assignment. Finally, on a Saturday in late 1983, George Abbey phoned her at home to see if she'd like to fly.

Excited to finally fulfill her childhood dream, Shannon said, "Of course!"

George didn't tell her much else, though. She'd have to keep the news to herself and wait to find out who her crewmates would be. Monday morning she went into the Johnson Space Center office she shared with fellow astronaut John Creighton, one of the people she most wanted to tell her news to.

The two had been office mates since they'd arrived at NASA and had formed a strong friendship. But John was acting strange that morning, as if hiding something. Shannon finally asked politely if he'd gotten a flight assignment. When he admitted he had, Shannon spilled the beans about hers, and learned they were on the same flight. Shannon couldn't have been more thrilled. Not only was she getting to fly but she'd be sharing the experience with a great friend.

They soon learned that their commander would be Dan Brandenstein, another TFNG, who'd already piloted a mission. John Fabian, who'd flown with Sally, would make his second flight. Pilot Steve Nagel would be a mission specialist on this trip. They were scheduled to launch in October 1984.

But just as Rhea's flight had gone through multiple changes, Shannon also saw her flight completely change in the years after she got the assignment. Originally it was supposed to carry a satellite and a special research lab. By the next year they were supposed to launch a big Syncom satellite and retrieve a spacecraft that had been in orbit for a few months. Payload specialists Charlie Walker and Greg Jarvis were now part of the crew.

A month before they were scheduled to fly, though,

and just after a big press conference about their mission, the crew learned that their flight had completely changed again. Changes made to flights ahead of them in the schedule had rippled down the line to their flight. Now Rhea's crew would take the Syncom satellite (ultimately leading to the space heist), and Shannon's would have a new payload. Different payload specialists, too. French medical researcher Patrick Baudry was added. Charlie would still fly with them, but Greg, to whom Shannon had grown close, was assigned to a later flight.

After all the uncertainty, Shannon's crew was finally set to fly mission STS-51-G in 1985. They would launch three communications satellites. One of those satellites, called Arabsat, was mostly funded by the Middle Eastern nation of Saudi Arabia to provide communications services for the nations of the Arab League. Along with it the crew would get another new payload specialist, one handpicked by Saudi Arabia to "oversee" the satellite's deployment.

While a newcomer entering the mix at the last minute might have made some feel slightly uneasy, there were also concerns about the satellite. "Arabsat had three safety reviews. It never passed any of them," John Fabian said. "Mr. Abbey didn't think we should fly it. I didn't think we should fly it. The flight controllers didn't think we should fly it. And the JSC Safety Office didn't think we should fly it. And yet, we flew it."

At the time, NASA was competing with Europe's main launch provider, Arianespace, to launch as many communications satellites as possible. According to John, boundless confidence had become part of NASA's identity. "NASA didn't make mistakes" back then, he said. "We were invincible."

So the crew pushed on, training for their entirely new mission in just three months' time.

When Shannon and her crewmates finally learned who the seventh crew member would be, they got a royal surprise.

Arabsat's overseer would be twenty-eight-year-old Sultan bin Salman Al Saud, a Saudi prince and nephew of the king. Sultan would be the first member of a royal family to fly in space as well as the youngest person to fly on the space shuttle. His biggest task in space would be to take pictures of Arabsat's release, and of Saudi Arabia and the Middle East.

Sultan had lived in the United States for much of the 1970s and spoke English fluently. He understood American culture. In fact, he sometimes understood jokes that Patrick, from France, didn't get until Sultan explained them. But Shannon was reserved with the prince at first. She wasn't a big fan of Saudi Arabian culture, especially when it came to the treatment of women, whose rights are severely limited in the kingdom. She kept her distance for the first few weeks of training, but over time she warmed to Sultan. They became friendly and professional, though never completely open with each other. Sultan came from a country where women never would have been considered for something like spaceflight at the time.

There were hiccups, but they came from the NASA managers and Saudi officials, who were desperate to avoid a culture clash, not from Sultan himself. The first involved echocardiograms. Patrick would be taking images of the heart similar to those Rhea had produced on her mission. Shannon would have her heart scanned with a specially designed device, but Patrick wanted more subjects. Shannon suggested Sultan, but NASA officials said no. The flight would have just one probe to use for the experiment, and a probe that touched a woman's skin couldn't then be used to touch a royal body.

Shannon felt a bit like she had been thrown back into the early days of her career. That feeling grew when she was advised not to wear shorts during the mission, so there wouldn't be too much of her legs showing when pictures were taken. This time, though, Shannon decided to ignore that recommendation. She was there to do her job, and she didn't care if what she wore offended anyone.

With the crew now in place, three weeks before the mission the crew members lay on their backs in their seats inside

Discovery. Rehearsals for launch could be tedious, involving plenty of long hours spent strapped to a hard metal seat. For all the exciting things astronauts got to do in flight, they did just as much waiting on the ground.

While they lay in the cockpit, John Creighton noticed that Shannon had her eyes closed. She was fast asleep, dreaming the time away. "We started talking quietly," John recalled, "and we kept saying, 'Do you think she's going to do that on launch morning?'"

Sure enough, when it came time to launch for real on June 17, Shannon again lay back in her cockpit seat for a short nap while waiting for the countdown clock to reach zero. That was just the way Shannon operated. She was cool, calm, and collected—a woman comfortable with her situation, so why not grab a little shut-eye before the real work began?

But ten minutes before the clock reached zero, Shannon's eyes were back open. She was wide awake as the space shuttle's engines ignited. The vehicle lurched off the launchpad and hurtled into the sky. Of all the things Shannon thought at the time, the two words that stood out were "at last."

"I mean, it was such a relief to think that you're actually on your way," she said, having dreamed of this moment when she was a little girl who, like Rhea, watched Sputnik sail across the sky.

During the first three days, Shannon and the other mission specialists released the three communications satellites. The operations were a breeze. Each satellite leisurely floated out into space and worked as expected.

On the fourth day Shannon put her robotic arm skills to work. Just as Sally and John Fabian had done, Shannon manipulated the arm to remove a payload from the cargo bay. It was the Shuttle Pointed Autonomous Research Tool for Astronomy (SPARTAN). Designed to study X-rays and the supermassive black hole at the center of the Milky Way, SPARTAN was a free-flying payload that weighed more than two thousand pounds. It would operate on its own for forty-five hours, disconnected from the shuttle's computers.

With ease Shannon lifted the SPARTAN out of the bay with the robotic arm, then dropped it into space to stare at our universe's most mysterious objects for the next forty-five hours. Throughout the process Shannon remained as relaxed and steady as always. "You never have to worry about whether or not something's going to be right, because Shannon is going to make it right," John said, looking back. "And that's not true of everybody. That's not true of some of the finest people I've known in my life." After the SPARTAN had fulfilled its role, the robotic arm was used to retrieve it and tuck it back into the bay.

While Shannon and the others did their work in orbit,

everyone on the ground was interested in Sultan. So many people were eager to see the royal in space that NASA scheduled the crew for a televised press conference on the last day of their mission. Once again NASA worried about its image. Pictures from the astronauts had come down to Earth, showing that Shannon had been wearing shorts. Now NASA fretted that Shannon's bare legs might float next to Saudi Arabian royalty on television.

An official message was sent to Mission Control in Houston, requesting that the crew wear pants for the press conference. Mike Mullane, who was serving as CAPCOM, saw the message. The man who had once called himself a sexist pig immediately threw the message into the trash.

Despite NASA's concerns, the press conference was just fine. Sultan said that his days in space had changed him. "Looking at it from here, the troubles all over the world and not just the Middle East look very strange as you see the boundaries and border lines disappearing."

As for Shannon's legs, they were out of the camera's frame the entire time.

STS-51-G was a nearly flawless mission. The crew returned home on time without any major trials. As Shannon put her feet back on Earth, she felt as if she'd doubled her weight. This feeling is common among those who return from the weightlessness of space to the gravity of our planet. "I

246 • THE SIX

thought, *Oh, my goodness, I feel so heavy,*" Shannon said. *"You mean, I have to live the rest of my life just like this?"*

The weighted feeling died down, and Shannon flew back to Houston to see her husband and children. As her youngest child ran up to her, Shannon braced herself for words of love. "Mom," he cried, "what are you going to cook for supper tonight? I'm so tired of pizza!"

Although the spaceflight had been smooth for Shannon, afterward things took a more dramatic turn. As part of the routine press tour after the flight, the crew traveled to cities throughout the United States and to France. A stop in Saudi Arabia was also planned, but that would prove vastly more complicated.

The schedules for Saudi Arabia had the men attending events together, while Shannon had separate activities. She reminded the trip planners that she was part of the crew and should be with the others whenever they appeared at events. There was also the issue of entering the country. At the time, any woman who visited Saudi Arabia had to have a designated male guardian or sponsor. The only way Shannon could make the trip was if the mission commander, Dan Brandenstein, served in that role for her. Shannon said no. She saw it as demeaning that she alone, as a woman, had to have a male sponsor to enter a country.

NASA came up with another idea. When Queen Elizabeth II had visited Saudi Arabia in 1979, the country had deemed her an "honorary man" so that she could dine and interact with the king. NASA approached Shannon, but she shut that idea down. "Absolutely not," Shannon said. "I am who I am. . . . There's no way I'm going to be an honorary male."

Ultimately NASA agreed that Shannon didn't have to go to Saudi Arabia and be an honorary male. Still, the decision was a bummer for her. She'd loved to travel since she was a child and always wanted to see new places. But she stuck to her principles and stayed home, while her crewmates jetted off to the Middle East without her.

When the crew arrived in Saudi Arabia, though, Sultan asked, "Where's Shannon?" Without going into too many details, John tried to explain that Shannon had decided she didn't want to come. The news didn't sit well with the royal family, especially Sultan's mother. She was throwing a lavish reception that she wanted Shannon to attend. Later the crew learned that King Fahd placed a call to the White House and got President Reagan on the phone.

The next morning Shannon was sitting at her desk when a NASA official called. He informed Shannon that she was leaving for Saudi Arabia in an hour. Shannon thought about it for a minute. She couldn't afford to lose her job by saying no. Her kids were getting older, and she needed to save money for their education.

"Well, I don't have a passport," Shannon replied.

She was told that everything would be provided for her. Shannon headed home to pack and called her husband, Michael, at work. "I'm headed out to Saudi Arabia," Shannon told him, making sure he'd be home on time to watch the kids.

Then things happened quickly. A car pulled into her driveway to take her to the airport, and the driver handed her a passport provided by NASA. At the airport another stranger walked Shannon to a gate, and the two boarded a plane bound for New York City. And there yet another stranger approached her and said, "Follow me." So Shannon found herself on a plane bound for Saudi Arabia, still with no idea of where to go or what to do when she got there.

By the time Shannon arrived in the Middle East, night had fallen. Wandering the arrival area, she noticed another man approaching her. "I just got a call that you're showing up," he said. "Where are you headed?"

"Beats me!" Shannon answered.

This man, an American who seemed to work at the consulate, told Shannon he thought she was supposed to attend an event with Sultan's mother. "How are you going to get there?" he asked.

"I don't know!" said Shannon. "I don't even know where I'm going."

Having spotted a Saudi man who was about to board

a small white private jet, Shannon's companion called out, "Hey, where are you going?"

"Riyadh."

"I think she needs to go to Riyadh. Can she fly with you?"

"Sure!"

Soon Shannon found herself having a lovely conversation with a Saudi businessman she'd just met on his private jet. He had a great command of English, and when he learned Shannon was a pilot herself, he let her take the controls of the plane for a while.

After Shannon and her new friend touched down in pitch-dark Riyadh, the strange journey continued. A limousine took her to what she assumed was a hotel. She put on one of the three outfits she'd brought and was whisked away to her next location, an opulent palace. The rest of her crew and their spouses were there. Among her friends she was able to relax slightly. She sat and chatted with them during a banquet—for hours. Later she learned that Sultan's mother was happy that she was there. Apparently she had fulfilled her duty to NASA.

The next day, after some much needed rest at her hotel, Shannon wondered how she'd get home. She had only about five dollars with her. But once again a car arrived and drove her to the airport. When she stepped aboard the plane, she'd been in Saudi Arabia for less than twenty-four hours.

Back in Houston, Shannon described the whirlwind trip to her daughters. "You mean you hitchhiked a ride on an airplane with a strange man that you didn't know?" they asked, aghast.

Shannon shrugged. In space or on the ground, it was her nature to go with the flow. "Well, you know, you do what you got to do."

Sending a Teacher to Space

A new chapter in the space shuttle program was announced in August 1984, and not every astronaut felt that it was a good idea. President Reagan declared, "I'm directing NASA to begin a search in all of our elementary and secondary schools and to choose as the first citizen passenger in the history of our space program one of America's finest—a teacher."

NASA had said for a long time that the space shuttle was much like a simple truck, one that ferried people and freight up to Earth orbit and down again. Anyone could ride safely, not just NASA astronauts. And after years of promoting this line, the agency was finally starting to follow through.

It had started with payload specialists, who by then had flown on many of the shuttle missions.

Although they had not received the same training for spaceflight as the astronauts, most of them had been scientists or engineers. They'd represented companies that made parts for the shuttle or made the satellites that it carried into orbit. Even the Saudi prince who had flown on Shannon's mission had been connected with the Arabsat satellite.

Now that Senator Jake Garn had flown in the shuttle, NASA was talking about flying other members of Congress, those who headed committees that determined how much money the agency would get from the government.

But the new nationwide search that Reagan announced would be different. For the first time a citizen with no connection to NASA or the space program would ride the shuttle. After that, NASA said, it would send the first journalist into space.

Plenty of astronauts thought this "anyone can fly" trend was moving in the wrong direction, though. A seat given to a payload specialist, a politician, or a civilian was one not being given to an astronaut who'd spent years training just to go to space. On top of that, some astronauts felt that NASA was making the mistake of believing its own hype. Not a single astronaut thought the shuttle was completely routine, with little chance of failure. Many worried about the safety risks of putting inexperienced riders in shuttle seats.

Yet the plan moved ahead, and the choice was made. Judy's second mission would be joined by the first teacher to fly to space. Out of more than eleven thousand applicants, NASA picked a social studies and history teacher from New Hampshire named Christa McAuliffe. Once Judy's crew got to space, Christa was going to give school lessons and do a few science experiments.

Almost instantly Christa was a media darling. Unlike Judy, who actively avoided the media, Christa appeared on a number of TV shows, including *The Tonight Show* with Johnny Carson, who had joked about women astronauts just a few years before. Christa's vibrant personality quickly made her a beloved public figure. The nation was eager to see her go to space.

CHAPTER TWENTY-ONE

Turning Point

At the end of 1985 the mood among the astronauts was bright.

All of the TFNGs—including each of the Six—had finally gone to space. A lucky few had already flown twice. Sally, Judy, Anna, Rhea, and Kathy had their next flight assignments too. Shannon had just flown, so she didn't yet have a new assignment, but it wouldn't be long.

The year had been huge for the space shuttle program. The astronauts had flown a total of nine flights in 1985, and 1986 promised to be even more epic, with up to twelve flights planned. To meet the challenge, NASA had more astronauts in the corps than ever. New recruits of both genders had joined the program in 1980 and 1984, and there were now eleven women in the mix.

Everyone could feel the electricity of change in the air. The space shuttle program was entering a new, more vibrant phase.

Change was also in the air for Sally, though most of it was happening far away from NASA and Houston. It began in 1984, when she went to Atlanta, Georgia, to give a speech. One of Sally's old friends from tennis, Tam O'Shaughnessy, lived in Atlanta.

While Sally had left the tennis world in college, Tam had gone on to play professionally in the early 1970s. When she'd retired from the sport, she'd studied biology and begun teaching eighth grade. Tam and Sally had reconnected briefly while Sally had been in graduate school at Stanford, and Sally had even invited Tam to the launch of STS-7, although they hadn't spent time together in Florida because Sally had been in quarantine. Still, the invitation had led them to pick up their friendship again over the phone.

So Sally and Tam arranged to meet for a meal in Atlanta after Sally's speech. As they talked about their tennis days, it felt as if no time had passed. By the end of the meal, Sally knew she wanted to keep seeing her old friend again and again.

Throughout 1984 and into 1985, Sally made trips to Atlanta to see Tam. They usually just took long walks around Tam's neighborhood, recalling their days in the junior tennis circuit or swapping knowledge about physics and biology. But whenever Tam told her friends that Sally was coming to town, they all noticed a little sparkle in Tam's eye.

Back in Houston, Sally's marriage to Steve was breaking down. He felt her becoming more distant, and then, in mid-1985, things worsened when she was assigned to her third flight. Once she was back in training, she and Steve barely saw each other. On a visit to Atlanta, Tam saw Sally looking at her with love—and Tam realized that she felt it too. Their new relationship continued to grow, and Sally knew her marriage would be coming to an end.

Sally was not the only one of the Six whose personal life was changing at the time. Judy had dated on and off during her time at NASA, but she had been on her own much of the time. Now she was regularly seeing a former navy pilot who had entered the astronaut program in 1984. Most of her focus, though, was on training for her next flight.

Early in 1985, Judy was assigned to her second mission, STS-51-L. The crew included three of her TFNG classmates: Dick Scobee as commander, and Ron McNair and Ellison Onizuka as her fellow mission specialists. Mike Smith, an astronaut from the 1980 class, would pilot his first spaceflight, and they'd also have payload specialist Greg Jarvis on board. The seventh member of the crew would be Christa McAuliffe, the first teacher to go to space.

Judy was one of the astronauts who had expressed concerns about non-scientists and non-astronauts being added to shuttle flights. But outwardly she showed only support for the newcomers, and for whatever NASA wanted her to do. Judy wanted to dedicate her life to space. If that meant agreeing to NASA's public relations stunts, so be it. She had found her true passion working for the space program and wanted a front-row seat to the grand adventures NASA was rolling out. She told friends that she was going to live on Mars someday. Coming from anyone else, it might have sounded silly, but anyone who knew Judy believed there was a chance she could make it happen.

Of course, Judy knew that Red Planet living was still many years off. For now she would have to be content with her seat on the space shuttle *Challenger*, sharing the ride with Christa. And as Judy trained with Christa, she softened a bit and took the newbie under her wing. Because Christa's teaching focus had been social studies, she struggled with the math and science she needed to learn before boarding the shuttle. Judy met her more than once for coffee, and gave her quick lessons and advice on how to make it through. Christa wrote to her parents that J.R. "especially had been very helpful."

But it was starting to feel as if Judy's second flight would never get off the ground. The mission was originally supposed to fly in November 1985, but it was delayed several times. Finally, on January 25, 1986, it seemed like they might be ready to fly the next day. Then a weather check showed bad conditions in the launch window on January 26, so NASA decided to delay again.

Everyone thought this decision was odd. Usually NASA would go ahead with the countdown, just in case the weather turned out to be okay. Weather in central Florida was always unpredictable. Sure enough, skies were clear on January 26, but the launch had already been postponed.

The crew finally headed out to the launchpad on January 27 and strapped in for flight. Then the strangest problem arose. The ground crew couldn't get the hatch door to close properly. By the time the problem was solved, strong winds had picked up near the pad. They ran out of time in their launch window, and the slightly grumpy crew left the shuttle. NASA would try yet again the next day.

But that night Judy and the rest of her crew didn't really believe they were going to launch the next day either. Weather forecasts predicted that temperatures would dip into the low twenties overnight. There was a general sense that it would be way too cold the next morning to launch. The astronauts went to bed not expecting to see space the next day.

As predicted, overnight the air above Cape Canaveral dropped to just twenty-four degrees Fahrenheit. Heaters were placed throughout the launchpad, but to keep the maze of pipes around *Challenger* from freezing, NASA engineers took the extra step of pumping water through the shuttle's fire suppression system. A worrying byproduct of this measure to keep the pipes warm was that drops of water trickled down the shuttle and its launchpad. As the air grew more frigid, the exposed water began to freeze. Despite the best efforts of the heaters, icicles hardened on the vehicle and the nearby service structure. When dawn came, the icicles glistened in the light, looking like thousands of bared teeth.

Still, Judy and the rest of the crew woke up at six a.m., almost half an hour earlier than they were supposed to. Because of the cold, NASA delayed the launch by an hour, but the crew couldn't sleep in. They were all feeling antsy, ready to go.

With plenty of time to spare, they shuffled into the dining room to eat breakfast, a time-honored tradition before every spaceflight. Steak and eggs were always on the preflight menu, and Judy was especially hungry for protein, so she chose two steaks and a generous portion of scrambled eggs.

After breakfast the crew huddled in a conference room for their final weather briefing. Flight controllers at the Johnson Space Center told them that, yes, it was cold and some ice had formed out on the launchpad. Crews had been out on the pad throughout the night, inspecting the ice and trying to remove some of the icicles for fear they might break off during launch and possibly damage *Challenger*.

But JSC didn't seem too worried. There was no sign

that the cold was a problem, so the crew left to suit up.

Soon, wearing her light blue flight suit, Judy stepped through the gray doors of the building that housed Cape Canaveral's astronaut crew quarters. The air was chilly, but the sky above was a crystal-clear blue. It seemed like a perfect day to launch. Judy waved to the gathered crowd as she walked toward the van that would carry her and the rest of the crew to the launchpad.

All the next steps felt like second nature to Judy at this point. She'd done them before, plenty of times for her first flight, and just yesterday for the flight that hadn't launched. There was the pull-up to the launchpad, followed by the elevator ride up to 195 feet. There was the long walk across the suspended walkway to reach the shuttle's cabin. (Though this time the crew had to step carefully so as to not slip on the icy path.) And there was the last look out at the Florida coast before entering the shuttle.

Admiring the clear blue sky, Dick Scobee reassured his crew, saying, "This is a beautiful day to fly."

Judy hopped around to stay warm before getting suited up with her headset and helmet. Next to her stood Christa, who'd be flying below her in the mid-deck. As Judy entered the cockpit, she turned to Christa and said, "Well, next time I see you we'll be in space!"

But first came the necessary waiting game.

"Kind of cold this morning," Ellison said over the

intercom. He was seated next to Judy and behind Mike, the pilot. Everyone knew that Ellison hated being cold, so Mike took the moment to tease him about his position just out of view of the main windows. "Up here, Ellison, the sun's shining in," Mike said over their headsets.

Flight controllers spoke into Judy's ear, asking her for a communications check. Feeling particularly amped that morning, she yelled, "COWABUNGA!"

As the support personnel strapped Christa in down below in the mid-deck, a gust of hot air suddenly blasted through the cabin. It was a gift from the closeout team to help warm the freezing crew.

The minutes ticked by. They all felt that familiar misery of lying on their backs in a hard metal seat for hours. Meanwhile the threat of another scrub hung over their heads. The idea of getting out of the shuttle and doing this same dance all over again another day seemed like an absolute nightmare. At T-minus nine minutes the countdown entered the planned hold, and they wondered if it would come out.

"I hope we don't drive this down to the bitter end again today," Judy said. Her excitement was beginning to fade.

But over the intercom Dick heard from flight controllers. They had reviewed the ice situation one last time, and the crew was officially a go for launch. "All right!" he yelled, and Judy did a quick calculation of liftoff time: 11:38 a.m.

The minutes disappeared one by one. With two minutes to go, Dick told his crew, "Welcome to space, guys."

At T-minus six seconds, the engines ignited as planned. Likely remembering how her first mission had been aborted on the launchpad, Judy waited to feel the rumble of the hardware starting to generate more than one million pounds of thrust.

"All right," she said with relief when she felt it. As the engines reached full thrust, again Judy cried, "All *right*!"

And then, liftoff. Judy had been here before. The vibrations, the sounds, the forces on her body—she knew exactly what to expect this time and braced herself for each milestone. Her crewmates all kicked into action, sounding out each step on the checklist while celebrating their launch.

"Houston, *Challenger*. Roll program," Dick said.

The shuttle twirled onto its back, just as it had done for every flight before.

It was Judy's turn. "LV, LH," she said fourteen seconds in, the same terms that Sally had barely managed to get out during her first flight.

"There's Mach 1," Mike called out at forty seconds. They were officially traveling faster than the speed of sound. Seventeen seconds later they increased the thrust of their engines, giving them more power to reach their final orbit. The crew shouted in jubilation.

Just over a minute into the flight, it was time to punch

up the engines again. Down in Mission Control, flight controllers gave *Challenger* the signal.

"*Challenger,* go at throttle up," Dick Covey, the CAP-COM on duty, said from the ground.

"Roger," Dick Scobee said.

Outside the space shuttle a bright flash appeared three seconds later. Then a jolt. Followed by a realization that something was wrong.

CHAPTER TWENTY-TWO
Endings and Answers

On the morning of Judy's second launch, Kathy was on her way home to Houston after an exhausting week in California. She'd been there to prepare for her next mission, which would carry into orbit a satellite called the Hubble Space Telescope, the largest telescope that had yet been launched into space, designed to make a variety of scientific observations and to be serviced over time by shuttle astronauts.

It was exciting work, but it had been a busy week. Kathy yawned. Realizing that she was much too tired to do anything useful, she called Jessie, her secretary, and started to explain why she wouldn't be coming in to work.

Kathy's words were met with a long, strange pause.

Then Jessie said in a shaking voice, "Didn't you hear what happened?"

That morning Rhea was in a conference room with the crew of her next scheduled mission, ready for a day of training. They found a TV to watch *Challenger*'s countdown and launch. Someone reminded them that their own mission had originally been scheduled for this time. This was supposed to have been their flight. And here was Rhea, watching with envy as Judy took flight for a second time while she waited to get back off the ground.

She saw the small black-and-white *Challenger* climb into the blue sky. Then a white cloud of flame and smoke engulfed the shuttle. Her voice uncertain, Rhea said that it was the booster rockets separating.

"No," a crewmate said. "It's too early."

Shannon was in training too, listening to a lecture in Mission Control. The lecturer suddenly stopped talking when a man ran into the control center, visibly upset.

"There's been a problem with the shuttle," he said.

Shannon ran out of the room in search of the nearest TV.

Meanwhile Anna was sitting on the flight deck of the shuttle mission simulator, practicing with the robotic arm for her mission just six weeks away. When Anna learned that *Challenger*'s countdown had started again after the planned hold at the nine-minute mark, she asked for the training simulation to be paused so that they could go watch the launch on TV.

Anna and her crewmate witnessed the same shocking

sight that Rhea saw miles away. They knew training was over for the day.

Sally had seen every launch of the space shuttle, either on TV or with her own eyes at the Cape. Or she'd been on them. But this time she was on a plane, traveling back to Houston from celebrating Tam's birthday in Atlanta. For the first time she'd miss seeing a launch.

A chime sounded over the speakers, signaling that the captain was about to speak. As Sally listened, her stomach dropped. There had been an accident, a major disaster, during the morning's shuttle launch. Sally's mind raced. She took her NASA ID badge up to the cockpit and told the crew that she was an astronaut.

The pilots let Sally into the cockpit and gave her an extra headset so she could listen to the updates that started to trickle in. The spacecraft had completely broken apart, according to reports. Sally suddenly realized that Judy and all her other friends aboard *Challenger* were gone. . . .

The astronauts gathered at the Johnson Space Center, stunned and grieving. None of them knew what to do. They just wanted to be there, to help if needed. There was also some small comfort in being around people who were going through the same thing. The military astronauts had suffered losses like this, watching a friend go in the blink of an eye. As devastated as those astronauts were by the shuttle disaster, the feelings were somewhat familiar. For the mission specialists, what had just happened was an entirely new kind of horror.

Sally couldn't stop thinking about Judy, who had been in the same seat Sally had sat in during her two flights. "When I visualize what's going on in the cockpit during that accident, it's actually from that perspective," Sally would later say. "From Judy's seat is where I picture, you know, what must have happened and what they . . . must have been going through."

For everyone the size of the loss was unimaginable. They hadn't just lost one friend. Seven people were gone in an instant: five astronauts and two payload specialists. Among them were four of the original TFNGs and one of the Six, who'd been America's second woman in space. And a teacher who'd planned to share her journey into space with students around the world.

Grief gripped the astronauts' hearts, and uncertainty hung heavy in the air. Underlying the sorrow, each of them thought the same thing, but they didn't dare say it: *Could this be the end of the space shuttle program?*

Three days later President Ronald Reagan stood before thousands of mourners on a lawn at the Johnson Space Center, honoring the memory of the astronauts who'd been lost. Most who were there hung their heads and wiped away tears. Families of the *Challenger* astronauts clutched one another for support.

Missing from the audience were Kathy and Sally, who had flown to Ohio to be present at a personal memorial for Judy at a synagogue. More than a thousand people showed up to pay their respects, double the temple's capacity. "Our Jewish tradition tells us that those who pioneer are partners with God," the rabbi overseeing the service told the crowd. "Judy heard an inner voice challenging her to climb higher. She heard a call to fly—to touch the sky. In that she excelled."

Once the service ended, the mourners spilled outside and looked at the sky. Four NASA jets flew overhead in the missing-man formation, spaced apart to make it seem as though one jet was absent. This traditional military salute to a fallen flier had been performed countless times. But this time the person missing was a woman.

Sally and Kathy huddled together with the women of the Resnik family as they extended their hands toward the jets, curling their fingers to make the American Sign Language sign for "I love you."

There they saluted Judy one last time.

Amid the outpouring of grief, though, was a growing question: What had gone wrong?

The day after Judy's memorial service, Sally was asked to serve on a fourteen-person presidential commission to find out why *Challenger* had exploded a little more than a minute after liftoff. The commission would be headed by William Rogers, who had been secretary of state under President Richard Nixon more than a decade earlier. Sally would be the only current astronaut on the panel, but it would include some of the biggest names in spaceflight, including former astronaut Neil Armstrong and test pilot Chuck Yeager. Richard Feynman, a scientist who'd helped develop the atomic bomb, would also be a member.

It was a lot to ask. Before the tragedy Sally had thought her time at NASA might soon come to an end, because she was considering a return to university life. But as she said to friends who were with her when she got the call, "I need to do this."

She didn't know then that the investigation's twists and turns would rival those of a thriller.

A little over a week later, Sally was in an office building next to the White House. She sat at a conference table with the other members of the commission—all men once again. This was their third meeting as an official group.

These meetings were fact-gathering sessions to help the commissioners better understand the events surrounding the *Challenger* launch. Sally and her team began by interviewing dozens of engineers and managers at NASA and at the shuttle's various contractors, putting together the pieces of what went wrong that day.

The sessions lasted hours and covered almost every topic imaginable. And Sally was always ready to ask a pointed, clarifying question. Soon the timeline of the accident began to take shape in the commissioners' minds.

The culprit had been the shuttle's right solid rocket booster. Specifically, the joints in the bottom of the booster—the thin rubber O-rings that sealed the big sections of the rocket together—had ruptured somehow. The break in the O-rings had let hot gases from inside the rocket come through its outer casing.

Flames had then quickly swelled through the open rift in the rings, hit the nearby external fuel tank, and caused it to leak a massive amount of flammable hydrogen. At that point a cascade of events took place in less than a second. As the external tank weakened, a strut connecting the solid rocket booster to the tank began to come loose. The booster spun and slammed into the tank. Fuel was released, and it ignited in the explosion they had all seen.

It had happened in a flash, before the crew could have reacted.

Another clue was soon spotted in footage of the take-off. A puff of black smoke spouted from the bottom of the right solid rocket booster at launch. It was there for just an instant, but it was more evidence to the committee that the O-rings had failed at their main job: keeping the pieces of the booster rocket sealed together.

Knowing all this was just part of the battle, though. The Rogers Commission couldn't pinpoint exactly *why* this failure had taken place. And to the commission's aggravation, every step of the way the press seemed to know more than NASA. Or at least the *New York Times* did.

Before the commission had even begun to suspect the O-rings, the paper reported that power and pressure in the right solid rocket booster had suddenly dropped just before the explosion. Then the paper published a blockbuster story claiming that the solid rocket boosters weren't designed to handle temperatures below forty degrees Fahrenheit—a red flag, given that it had been cold in Florida on the day *Challenger* launched. Sally and her fellow commissioners asked mission managers if the cold was to blame, but they were told only that it was one of many factors being considered.

Four days later the *Times* was back with another scoop. Apparently the paper had gotten hold of memos from someone at NASA. The documents showed that a staff member there had previously voiced concerns about O-rings breaking one day, leading to a major catastrophe.

So NASA had known that the O-rings might be an issue. Blown away by this knowledge, the Rogers Commission decided to hold a closed-door meeting to get to the bottom of the matter. But as the day wore on, the discussions became exceptionally dull. Sally did her best to listen as a speaker went into great detail about the joints in the solid rocket boosters.

During a break she returned a call from a reporter at the *Washington Times*. He'd heard a rumor that, before launch, a contractor had expressed concern to NASA regarding the cold temperatures. Sally was surprised. She decided to get to the bottom of this rumor. When she returned to the meeting, she asked, "Is there any internal correspondence on potential concern over the operation of the O-ring or the joint?"

Sally's goal was to connect the dots. She wanted to see if maybe there was a link between the cold temperatures and the failure of the O-rings, and if NASA had talked about such a possibility. The man who'd been speaking about the boosters said that there'd been a meeting the night before the launch, and that engineers had discussed the possibility of problems due to the cold. But they'd decided to move forward with the mission. "We all concluded that there was no problem with the predicted temperatures," he said.

Sally asked him about the NASA memos that had been described in the newspaper article. He said he wasn't aware of any such documents. The meeting went on.

Then a man from the back of the room walked up to the main conference table. He was Allan McDonald from Morton Thiokol, the company that manufactured the solid rocket boosters. As the commission members looked at him with some confusion, he said in a shaking voice, "I wanted to say a point about the meeting."

He meant the last-minute meeting on the night before takeoff, the meeting at which everyone had supposedly agreed that the cold wouldn't be a problem. Then Allan dropped a bomb.

He and others at Morton Thiokol had originally recommended just before the flight not launching in temperatures below fifty-three degrees Fahrenheit. They had data that showed that as the O-rings became colder, they also became less flexible.

These words were met with stunned silence.

The commission chairman asked Allan to repeat himself. As he did so, the mood in the room shifted. The commissioners were realizing that there *had* been concern about the cold. And that engineers had advised NASA not to launch *Challenger*.

It was sometime after that session that Sally stared at a paper she held in her hands. It was marked as an official NASA document, and it had two columns of figures. One listed temperatures. The second listed the resiliency, or flexibility, of the O-rings at each of those temperatures. The numbers held the key to what had happened to *Challenger*.

The document showed that as the temperature dropped, the O-rings became stiffer and stiffer. But the O-rings only worked by staying flexible, so that they could keep a tight seal in the gaps between the parts of the booster rockets during flight. Stiffness meant the O-rings could become brittle and break. Stiffness meant death.

How the document made its way into Sally's hands is a mystery to this day. Someone associated with NASA gave it to her, but no one has publicly claimed responsibility for it. Steve always suspected it was one of NASA's contractors. Tam was certain it was an employee at the Johnson Space Center who knew that Sally would stand up for what was right. "Sally had this reputation at NASA and other places, just that she was a person of integrity and that she had a scientific mind," Tam said. "She couldn't be swayed by politics or that sort of thing."

Sally never revealed the source of the leak, knowing it could have ended someone's career. She also knew that if she went public with the information herself, people might be able to trace it back to the original leaker. So she decided to quietly hand off the information to someone else on the Rogers Commission. She chose Don Kutyna, a general who oversaw space systems for the air force. Sally had liked Don from the start. She felt he was a man of integrity who could be trusted to do the right thing with the precious document. So one afternoon, as the two of them walked down a hallway, Sally handed Don the piece of paper without saying a word, then walked away.

Don grasped the seriousness of the numbers, but he decided to pass this information to another commission member, one with fewer ties to the government. He settled on the physicist Richard Feynman, who was known for unconventional behavior. Feynman would understand the science, and he wouldn't be afraid to speak out about it, loudly.

So the general invited the physicist over for dinner and took him out into the garage to see his car. Don removed the car's carburetor—a piece of equipment sometimes used to control the flow of fuel and air into an engine—and pretended to clean it.

"Professor, these carburetors have O-rings in them," he said. "And when it gets cold, they leak." Richard Feynman didn't say a word, but a light bulb flicked on in his mind. Of course cold makes the O-rings stiff, and when they become stiff, they could potentially break and fail. The two finished the night with no more talk of O-rings.

The next meeting of the Rogers Commission had audience members and camera crews present. At the meeting Richard asked for a cup of ice water, but he didn't drink it. And when the commissioners passed around a model of a solid rocket booster joint, Richard kept it in front of him, next to the ice water. He took out a pair of pliers, removed the O-ring from inside the seal, and put it into his ice water. And then he waited. When the O-ring was cold, he pressed the button to turn his microphone on.

Richard pulled the O-ring out of his ice water and addressed the speaker who had earlier downplayed the role of temperatures in the O-ring failure.

"I took this stuff that I got out of your seal and I put it in ice water," he said, "and I discovered that when you put some pressure on it for a while and then undo it, it doesn't stretch back."

A scientist had just shown what had doomed *Challenger*. O-rings lose their flexibility when they get cold. It was a small science experiment that Richard Feynman would become famous for. But it began with a vital piece of information passed to Sally Ride, who played a key part in making the truth public.

While Sally helped crack the case of the O-rings, the other four remaining women of the Six did whatever it took to keep the space program afloat. Once it was clear that none of the shuttles would see space in the near future, the astronauts were assigned to go through every checklist and document related to past flights. Often NASA had listed multiple ways of doing certain tasks, or held duplicate documents, and the hope was that making the process more efficient might lower risks to future flights. "It was a lot of long, long hours, sitting, going line by line, through every single piece of documentation," said Shannon. And they did it for months.

Then came a mission that no one had expected—not in space but at sea.

Everyone at NASA had assumed the *Challenger* crew had died instantly in the blast, vaporized in seconds. It was tragic, but there was some comfort in knowing that their deaths had been quick. As experts analyzed the footage of the launch in the weeks after the disaster, though, they made a grim discovery: a small white speck trailing away from *Challenger's* destruction, heading toward the sea. It was the crew cabin.

One of the biggest underwater searches in history began. NASA drew help from the military and various agency contractors. Dozens of ships, aircraft, and submarines—along with thousands of rescue personnel—scoured the depths of the ocean floor, hoping to find where the crew had returned to Earth.

After almost six weeks, divers found the remains of the cabin and the crew. Under the cloak of darkness one night, the recovered remains were shipped to port. Hoping to show respect, someone had draped American flags over the containers carrying the crew. This alerted the press, and photographers snapped some pictures. Soon the world knew that the *Challenger* astronauts had been found.

NASA's investigation into the final moments of the *Challenger* crew found evidence that the astronauts had survived the breakup of the shuttle long enough to turn on emergency oxygen supplies. Ultimately, though, there was no way to know if the crew had been conscious when they'd hit the water.

Meanwhile, the Rogers Commission finished its investigation and turned in its final report on June 9, 1986. The massive four-hundred-fifty-page document changed NASA forever. It detailed NASA's troubled history with the solid rocket boosters' O-rings. Before *Challenger*, up to seven flights had experienced some form of O-ring erosion, including Judy's first flight. And many of the problems had happened at colder temperatures.

The report was a stinging criticism of NASA's safety procedures. The agency's pressure to increase the pace of flights might have contributed to corners being cut. The commission recommended almost a complete overhaul of how NASA did business. It even suggested that satellites should return to being launched on uncrewed rockets.

Clearly things were going to change.

After the Disaster: Accountability and Honor

Tragically, a number of family members and other loved ones of the people aboard *Challenger* witnessed the explosion from the roof of the Launch Control Center. Among them were Judy's father, Marvin, and her brother, Chuck.

For a little over a minute after the shuttle launched, Marvin was filled with nothing but pride for his space-bound daughter. Then came the flash, the enormous cloud billowing out from where the shuttle had been, and the sound of the explosion. In the moments after that terrible shock, people on the roof began to yell and sob, but it was the cries of the children that would stick with Marvin for years to come.

After the cause of the incident was known, NASA had to make things right for the families of those who'd been lost. Because Judy Resnik had died unmarried and without children, NASA was reluctant to offer her family a cash settlement comparable to those the other families would receive. To Marvin this was unacceptable. His daughter's life was as valuable as the other astronauts'. He found help in Michael Oldak, who was both Judy's former husband and a lawyer. Michael said, "Judy put me through law school. I'll do this for them." In the end Judy's family received a settlement that Michael felt was appropriate.

The *Challenger* tragedy brought upheaval to NASA and to many families, but a light did emerge from the darkness. June Scobee, whose husband, Dick, had been the mission commander, dreamed of a living memorial for the crew. That dream came true in the form of the Challenger Center for Space Science Education, a nonprofit created in 1986 to inspire kids to pursue careers in STEM. Founded by the families, it has headquarters in Washington, DC. It now operates centers in schools, museums, and other institutions around the country. Both Marvin and Chuck Resnik have served on its advisory council.

CHAPTER TWENTY-THREE
Going On

After the disastrous loss of *Challenger*, NASA and the five remaining members of the Six found ways to move forward, but not always together.

Two questions loomed huge after the explosion. What had caused it? And should the space shuttle program continue?

While the Rogers Commission answered the first question, thanks to Sally's key contribution, for a time the answer to the second was unclear. It wasn't certain that any American, man or woman, would travel to space again. Many people feared that the loss of *Challenger* would end the space shuttle program. It might even end NASA's mission of space exploration. But the agency kept going through one of the most difficult times in its history to that point.

The fate of *Challenger* and its crew was a wake-up call for NASA, a chance for the agency to learn from past mistakes. NASA reviewed safety procedures and redesigned the shuttle to make it safer for astronauts. Future astronauts would wear orange pressure suits that would keep the crew alive for a while if their spacecraft lost air or pressure. NASA also dropped plans to send non-astronauts into space and eased the pressure to make more frequent flights. More than two and a half years would pass before the next space shuttle mission took five astronauts, all men, into space aboard *Discovery*.

By that time America's best-known woman astronaut was no longer an astronaut.

Sally had begun to change her life even before the *Challenger* disaster. In late 1985 she and Steve had agreed to divorce, although they kept that decision to themselves for a while, and she felt that her third mission, when it came, would be her last. But once her work on the Rogers Commission ended, Sally was ready to start the next chapter of her life. She didn't want to leave NASA just yet, though, with the wounds of *Challenger* not fully healed, so she offered to work out of NASA's Washington, DC, headquarters, which ended her time as an astronaut.

While working in Washington, Sally carried out one final, important project for NASA. With the space shuttle fleet temporarily grounded, the agency found itself in need of direction. Sally was asked to form a planning group that would come up with a bold framework for NASA's future. She and her team spent nearly a year developing a new path for NASA. In 1987 they turned in what became known as the Ride Report. It recommended four major goals for NASA.

The most ambitious goals were to create an outpost on the moon, and then send humans to Mars. NASA still hopes to achieve these goals. The next most important goal was to use robots and uncrewed spacecraft to further explore the planets, moons, and other bodies in our solar system. Through many missions—including landing robotic rovers on Mars and sending probes on years-long voyages to photograph and observe more distant planets and their moons—NASA's planetary science program has made a lot of progress on this front.

The fourth item on the list was something new: Mission to Planet Earth. This was a call for NASA to launch satellites that would observe Earth from space, measuring how the planet's weather and climate changed over time. Ever since the life-altering moment when Sally had gazed from space at the fuzzy blue atmosphere of Earth, she had known that this atmosphere needed protecting. Even though NASA yearned to strike out beyond humans' home planet, she urged the agency to turn its sights inward and study that blue planet.

Mission to Planet Earth was a controversial suggestion. Not only was it a completely different direction for NASA, but not everyone wanted to expand research into issues such as climate change. At first NASA considered burying

Mission to Planet Earth. Sally thought it might even lead to her being fired, so she decided to control her own destiny. After turning in her report, Sally retired from NASA in 1987 and packed her bags for California. There she began a two-year fellowship at Stanford's Center for International Security and Arms Control, and her trips to Atlanta would continue. After her stint at Stanford, she went on to teach at the University of California San Diego.

Sally did maintain a relationship with NASA, though. She helped with the investigation after a second space shuttle disaster when *Columbia* broke up while reentering the atmosphere in 2003. She was asked twice to be NASA's administrator, but she turned down the job.

Instead Sally's main focus after her NASA years was connecting with people about science and space. In addition to university teaching and public speaking, she realized that she most loved speaking with children, and she also thought they asked the best questions. She worked on projects called EarthKAM and MoonKAM, which let children take pictures from cameras orbiting around Earth and the moon. But by far her biggest passion was a nonprofit company she created with Tam. Called Sally Ride Science, it uses space as a way to inspire kids, especially girls, to pursue careers in science and math.

Throughout their decades as life and business partners, Sally and Tam never made their relationship public. Then, on July 23, 2012, Sally died of cancer. Writing on the Sally Ride Science website, Tam called herself Sally's "partner of 27 years." Although some people had been aware of the relationship, Tam's statement went viral. It revealed Sally as the first publicly known LGBTQ astronaut.

Some people reacted with criticism, but the outpouring of love and support drowned out the negativity. "I have heard from people—friends, journalists, and other folks—who said that hearing that Sally and I were a couple made a huge difference in their coming out and being who they really are," Tam said. Sally's role as a pioneer had grown even after her death.

The *Challenger* accident powerfully reverberated across the personal and professional lives of Anna, Rhea, Kathy, and Shannon as well.

For Anna Fisher it meant that her 1984 mission—when she had helped rescue a satellite—was the only spaceflight she'd take. She had been scheduled for a second mission, but after the tragedy, flights were postponed and crew assignments were uncertain. Instead, in 1987, Anna Fisher sat at a conference table with NASA officials and managers. Nearly ten years after she'd been interviewed by the astronaut selection board, she was about to experience the whole process again, but this time she'd be doing the interviewing and selecting.

NASA was beginning to gear up for its return to flight with the space shuttle, but that was at least a year away. With so much uncertainty surrounding NASA's future, some people questioned the need to hire more space-farers. Others figured the agency needed to keep numbers up. They didn't know how many astronauts would leave NASA in the aftermath of the *Challenger* disaster.

Anna and the rest of the panel narrowed the list to fifteen finalists. Among them were the next two women who would become astronauts. One of them, Mae Jemison, would make history as the first Black woman selected to the astronaut ranks. It had taken decades, but NASA had finally learned an important lesson: courage and perseverance in the most pressure-filled situations are traits that don't belong to a single gender or race.

After taking a leave of absence from NASA to focus on raising her family, Anna returned to the agency in 1996 and played an important role in the early stages of developing the International Space Station, which was put together in Earth's orbit beginning in 1998. At one point Anna thought she might go to space for a second time, until the tragedy of *Columbia* put flights on hold again for several years. Ultimately Anna retired from NASA in 2017 after nearly forty years. "I was disappointed to not fly again," she said, "but I also realized how lucky I was." Being one of the few astronauts ever to have flown to space, she declared, "is a truly humbling experience."

Rhea Seddon also remained at NASA. She flew two more shuttle missions. Ever since joining the program, Rhea had wanted to do science in space. On her third and last mission, she was in charge of all science experiments performed during the flight. She ultimately left NASA in 1997 and returned to her home state of Tennessee and to her medical career. By then her husband, Hoot Gibson, had also retired from NASA after five space shuttle missions.

Kathy Sullivan flew two more space shuttle flights. One of them was the mission she'd been training for before the *Challenger* accident—the launch of the Hubble Space Telescope, which is still making important observations and photos of the universe to this day.

Kathy's government service then went beyond NASA. In 1988 she was commissioned to the US Naval Reserve as an oceanographer with the rank of lieutenant commander, returning to her first scientific passion, the study of the sea. Five years later she was named chief scientist of the National Oceanic and Atmospheric Administration (NOAA). She became the agency's administrator in 2014.

And Kathy's dream of exploring the earth's deepest waters came true. She took trips on submersibles, the small submarine-like vessels used for ocean exploration, and in 2020 she voyaged to Challenger Deep, the lowest known location on the planet. Kathy became the first woman to make the trip. She's the only person to have walked in space *and* traveled to the sea's deepest depths.

As for Shannon Lucid, who'd built her own spaceship out of cardboard boxes as a kid, she was the last of the Six to fly, but she spent more time in space than the rest combined. She flew four more shuttle missions after the *Challenger* disaster. Her most notable trip to orbit was in 1996, when she flew to Mir, a Russian space station.

Instead of returning to Earth with the rest of her shuttle crew, Shannon's mission called for her to stay on Mir for six months. She spent most of that time with two cosmonauts who spoke no English, so she used the Russian she'd studied for a year before the flight.

Shannon's stay aboard Mir was both deeply fulfilling and challenging. One minor complication was that her daughters had given her a science-fiction book to pass the time, but it ended on a major cliff-hanger! Without a bookstore nearby in space, she stewed over what would happen next, until the second volume arrived at the station on a cargo flight. In spite of such issues, Shannon learned that she preferred living in space over conducting short visits. When she returned to Earth from Mir, she had spent more time in space than any other American or any other woman. She held those records until 2007.

In the years after the Six left their mark on NASA and the world, the number of women astronauts grew. Every astronaut class since the historic 1978 group has included women. And these women have continued to make history.

Mae Jemison became the first Black woman astronaut and first woman of color in space in 1992 when she flew aboard the space shuttle *Endeavour.* Eileen Collins made history in 1995 when she became the first woman to pilot a space shuttle. Four years later she became the first female commander of a shuttle mission. Peggy Whitson became the first female commander of the International Space Station in 2007.

Still, NASA and the rest of the spacefaring world have a long way to go to reach equal representation. Of the more than six hundred people who've gone to space, less than one sixth have been women. Hopefully, that fact will be out of date soon. For women of color the representation is even more pitiful. Only five Black women have gone to orbit. The first Hispanic woman, Ellen Ochoa, flew to orbit in 1993, and only one other has followed. The first Indigenous woman, Nicole Aunapu Mann, went to space in 2022.

Meanwhile, NASA's decades-old decisions about women in space still affect those who go to space today, as shown by a space suit crunch. In March 2019, NASA announced plans for the first all-women space walk, which would happen outside the International Space Station. But before the astronauts were set to step outside the air lock, one of the women, Anne McClain, realized that a medium-sized suit would fit her best. At the time the space station had only larges and one medium prepared for use. So Anne bowed out, giving the medium to her female crewmate, who performed the space walk with a male astronaut.

The incident caused an uproar among those who'd looked forward to the historic moment. It also shone a light on NASA's space suit decisions, dating back to when the first six women had joined the agency all those years before. Smaller-sized space suits had not been made a priority over the years, which kept many smaller women from performing space walks. Astronaut Jessica Meir pointed out that "sometimes the effects of those decisions made back in the '70s carry over for decades to come." NASA didn't take long to make things right, though. Later that same year Jessica and her best friend and fellow astronaut, Christina Koch, stepped out of the International Space Station on the first all-female space walk.

Looking back on the importance of the Six, Eileen Collins said, "They didn't have any women [astronaut] role models. They were doing it for the first time. For those of us who followed, we had the role models. So that made us more comfortable, more confident, and more welcome."

This was certainly true for Eileen, who was training as a pilot at Vance Air Force Base in Oklahoma when the Six visited the base for their parachute survival training.

Though Eileen's first passion had been flying, she'd also been fostering the idea of becoming an astronaut. Just as young Shannon had noticed that all the Mercury Seven astronauts on that magazine cover were men, Eileen had read about the Gemini astronauts when she was in fourth grade, and noticed the same thing. So when the Six showed up at Vance, Eileen recalled years later, "Just the fact that they were on the same base I was on was very exciting. I thought, *This is something that I'm going to do someday.*"

Space travel has begun to look very different from when the Six came to NASA. Originally human space exploration was controlled by NASA and other government agencies. Now the commercial space industry is growing, with more opportunities for women and people of color to find their way to space without government approval. Several companies promise quick trips to the edge of space for customers who can pay their way. One such customer was Wally Funk, one of the thirteen women who'd passed the astronaut tests back in 1961 but had not been allowed to become astronauts. Sixty years later, in 2021, she flew on a Blue Origin rocket to the edge of space and back.

But NASA is still moving forward too, and women will be an essential part of its next chapter. In 2017 the agency announced the creation of the Artemis program to send humans back to the moon for the first time in more than half a century. Artemis, named after a goddess in Greek mythology, will strive to send the first woman and the first person of color to the lunar surface.

In April 2023, NASA took a major step toward keeping that promise. Christina Koch, one half of the first all-female space walk, and Victor Glover were assigned to the first crewed Artemis mission, which will loop around the moon. When they fly, Christina will become the first woman and Victor the first person of color to travel to deep space, beyond Earth's orbit.

And after them the world will learn of the next woman to make space history. One of NASA's current astronauts will be the first woman to walk on the moon. All she's waiting on is to be chosen.

AUTHOR'S NOTE

I'm beyond thrilled to bring the story of the Six to young readers. When the adult book was first published, I had the pleasure of traveling the country to speak to various audiences about these women's stories. And one thing that stood out to me was just how much their narratives still resonate with young women to this day, forty years later. The Six might have had extraordinary job titles, but their experiences, emotions, and triumphs are so familiar and relatable. They all began as kids with big dreams, just like many of you.

One thing I hope you'll discover with this book is the power of perseverance and self-confidence. Throughout their lives the Six often encountered closed doors or naysayers who did not believe they were capable of succeeding in fields long dominated by men. If they had listened to that negativity, they might not have found themselves orbiting Earth. Their story shows us how important it is to believe in your own strengths and abilities, especially when others do their best to make you doubt what you can achieve.

Another detail I love about the women of the Six is that they all had very different journeys that led them to space. Within the group there were two doctors, an astrophysicist, an electrical engineer, a chemist, and an oceanographer and geologist. And to this day more people are coming to NASA's astronaut programs from unexpected professions. Additionally the Six weren't all space cadets from the start. Half of the women held lifelong dreams of going to space one day, but the other half did not really consider the career of being an astronaut until the opportunity was presented to them. It's proof that there is no one true path to achieving your goals, even if those goals are blasting off from Earth, and proof that it's okay to take some time to figure out what you want to do in life, or be open to paths you may not have considered yet. When I was young, I sometimes felt like a failure for not knowing exactly what I wanted to do when I grew up, while everyone around me seemed to have some kind of calling from the moment they were born. It's fine to know—and not know—what lies ahead, as well as explore detours that materialize in front of you. Just think about Kathy, who was so certain she'd major in a foreign language, only to find joy in the pursuit of oceanography and geology!

For those of you interested in space, exciting times are on the horizon. NASA's Artemis program has the United States—and even the world—focused on returning to the moon in the years to come. And with the stated goal of sending a woman to the lunar surface, the Artemis program is putting women top of mind. And because these ambitious programs take many years to come to fruition, there will be plenty of opportunities for young readers like you to get involved as you grow up, and in the decades to come. But even if you want to keep your feet firmly on the earth's surface, I hope you'll be inspired by these extraordinary six women as you find your own path, dream your own dreams, and persevere through any challenges that come your way.

TIME LINE

1943 January 14, Shannon Lucid is born

1947 November 8, Margaret "Rhea" Seddon is born

1949 April 5, Judy Resnik is born

August 24, Anna Fisher is born

1951 May 26, Sally Ride is born

October 3, Kathy Sullivan is born

1955 Young Shannon reads an article about cosmonauts and space travel

1957 October, Rhea's father shows her Sputnik in the night sky

1960 Jerrie Cobb is tested for spaceflight fitness; other women pilots are tested in 1961

1961 May 5, Alan Shepard becomes the first American in space with his fifteen-minute flight; Anna is inspired to be an astronaut when she listens to the radio broadcast

1962 July 17, Jerrie Cobb and Janey Briggs Hart try to convince Congress and NASA to allow women to be astronauts; they are turned down

1963 June 16, Valentina Tereshkova of the Soviet Union becomes the first woman in space

1976 July 8, NASA announces that mission specialists will be recruited for the space shuttle program; for the first time women and minorities are welcome

1977 Nichelle Nichols makes a recruiting video for the space shuttle program

1978 January 16, George Abbey announces the selection of thirty-five new astronauts, including the Six

1979 Problems with *Columbia* delay the first shuttle launch by two years; Kathy sets a high-altitude flight record

1981 April 12, *Columbia* makes the first shuttle flight from Cape Canaveral

May 30, Rhea Seddon and Hoot Gibson become the first astronauts to marry in the astronaut corps

1982 April 19, Sally is selected for the seventh shuttle mission and Guion Bluford, the first Black astronaut in space, for the eighth

July, astronauts Sally Ride and Steve Hawley marry

August 19, cosmonaut Svetlana Savitskaya becomes the second woman to fly in space

1983 February, Judy learns that she will be the second American woman in space, on the first *Discovery* flight

June, Sally goes up in STS-7 for a six-day mission that lands in CA, not FL; by the end of the year, all of the Six have flown or received flight assignments

1984 July, cosmonaut Svetlana Savitskaya becomes the first woman to go to space twice and the first woman to spacewalk

August–September, Judy goes up for STS-41-D

October, Kathy and Sally go up for STS-41-G

November, Anna goes up for STS-51-A

1985 Judy is assigned to her second mission, STS-51-L

April, Rhea's mission, STS-51-D, flies after many delays

June, Shannon goes up for STS-51-G with the Saudi prince

1986 January, *Challenger* explodes after liftoff, killing all aboard—Francis R. (Diock) Scobee, Michael Smith, Judy Resnik, Christa McAuliffe, Ronald McNair, Ellison Onizuka, and Gregory Jarvis

June, the commission on which Sally served turns in the report on the *Challenger* disaster; Sally leaves the astronaut corps

1987 The Ride Report on the future of NASA, containing Sally's Mission to Planet Earth, is submitted; Sally retires from NASA; new astronauts are being selected

THE SIX: QUICK REFERENCE

Sally Ride

Born May 26, 1951. Hometown: Encino and Van Nuys, California. Education: PhD, master's, and bachelor's in physics, bachelor's in English, Stanford. Junior tennis champion. Accepted as NASA astronaut 1978. First American woman to fly in space. Veteran of two shuttle missions. Member of the Rogers Commission investigating the *Challenger* explosion, as well as the board that investigated the *Columbia* disaster.

Judy Resnik

Born April 5, 1949. Hometown: Akron, Ohio. Education: PhD in electrical engineering, University of Maryland; bachelor's in electrical engineering, Carnegie Mellon. Accepted as NASA astronaut 1978. Second American woman to fly in space, and first Jewish American to fly in space. Died while flying aboard *Challeng*er.

Kathy Sullivan

Born October 3, 1951. Hometown: born in Paterson, New Jersey, grew up in Woodland Hills, California. Education:

PhD in geology, Dalhousie University; bachelor's in earth sciences, University of California, Santa Cruz. Accepted as NASA astronaut 1978. Third American woman to fly in space. First American woman to walk in space. Veteran of four shuttle missions, including the launch of the Hubble Space Telescope. The only person to have walked in space and traveled to the deepest part of the ocean.

Anna Fisher

Born August 24, 1949. Hometown: born in St. Albans, New York, grew up in San Pedro, California. Education: doctor of medicine, master's and bachelor's in chemistry, University of California, Los Angeles. Accepted as NASA astronaut 1978. Fourth American woman to fly in space, and first mother to fly in space. Flew one shuttle mission.

Margaret "Rhea" Seddon

Born November 8, 1947. Hometown: Murfreesboro, Tennessee. Education: doctor of medicine, University of Tennessee; bachelor's in physiology, University of California, Berkeley. Accepted as NASA astronaut in 1978. Fifth American woman to fly in space. Veteran of three shuttle missions.

Shannon Lucid

Born January 14, 1943. Hometown: born in Shanghai, China, grew up in Bethany, Oklahoma. Education: PhD and master's in biochemistry, bachelor's in chemistry, University of Oklahoma. Accepted as NASA astronaut in 1978. Sixth American woman to fly in space. Veteran of five spaceflights. At one time held the record for longest continuous stay in space by an American and by a woman.

SOURCES

This book is the culmination of more than one hundred hours of interviews (mostly over Zoom during the COVID-19 pandemic) conducted between 2020 and 2022. Among the people I was grateful to talk to were Augusta Gonzalez, Barbara Roduner, Bill Colson, Robert Crippen, Bonnie Dunbar, Carolyn Huntoon, Charlie Walker, Dan Brandenstein, David Leestma, Duane Ross, Eileen Collins, Fani Brown Brandenburg, Frank Hughes, George Abbey, Gerald Griffin, Hoot Gibson, Jay Honeycutt, Jeff Hoffman, John Creighton, John Fabian, June Scobee Rodgers, Lynn Sherr, Margaret Weitekamp, Marianne Dyson, Michael Cassutt, Michael Oldak, Mike Mullane, Rhea Seddon, Rick Hauck, Shannon Lucid, Steve Hawley, Sue Okie, Taibi Kahler, Tam O'Shaughnessy, and Wayne Hale.

While I was not able to speak with Anna Fisher directly due to her contractual obligations, I was able to attend her various public presentations and Q&A events, which enabled me to ask detailed questions in public forums. In particular, at Kennedy Space Center's Chat with an Astronaut event, over the course of multiple presentations, I was able to obtain Anna's answers to many of my more pressing questions. I wasn't able to speak with Kathy Sullivan because she, too, was bound by precluding contractual obligations.

A pillar of my research was Johnson Space Center's Oral

History Project, which inspired me to write this book in the first place. Owing to the tireless efforts of JSC's historians, the project now contains interviews with roughly one thousand participants, including hours of interviews with former astronauts and major NASA personnel. All of the Six, except for Judy Resnik, gave interviews for the project, and they were unreserved in their answers and tales. For that I'm grateful.

Through the Freedom of Information Act, I received from NASA audio and video footage of old interviews with the Six, as well as video of the preflight press conferences for Sally's and Judy's first missions. I also obtained a video of an in-flight press conference that Anna Fisher's crew had conducted.

I obtained transcripts and NASA documents from the University of Houston–Clear Lake's JSC archive, which holds old biographies, documents related to astronaut selection, and materials corresponding to each of the Six's inaugural flights. I also transcribed hours of space-to-ground audio from the Six's Shuttle flights, which are available on Archive.org. I pulled details from years of chronologies and press releases out of Johnson Space Center and Kennedy Space Center, including the JSC Roundups—monthly internal memos sent to NASA personnel. NASA also holds extensive press kits of the original Shuttle missions.

Tam O'Shaughnessy graciously gave me invaluable audio journals recorded by Sally Ride herself, in which she detailed her time on the Space Shuttle and her trips to Europe following her history-making mission. The National Air and Space Museum also holds many of Sally's old notes and notebooks, which proved immensely useful.

I scoured the New York Public Library's archives and obtained hundreds of newspaper articles and magazine stories about the Six, many of which included interviews with the women when they were first selected. I have more than a hundred archived TV news stories from ABC, NBC, and CBS that report on the Six's flights and accomplishments, sourced from Vanderbilt University's Television News Archive. I also pulled from the Johnny Carson archive and *The Dick Cavett Show*.

The Six is merely a snapshot of the lives of these six incredible women. To truly do justice to their stories, six separate books would be required, but I was only contracted for one. Fortunately, many rich texts appeared before mine which offer wonderful insight into these women's lives, many of which I greatly relied on for context and details.

A few of the Six themselves have taken to writing their stories. Rhea Seddon's *Go for Orbit* is a fantastic, unflinching account of her time at NASA, and I found myself thumbing through my signed copy multiple times throughout the writing process to better understand her emotions at critical points. Kathy Sullivan's *Handprints on Hubble* was also invaluable reading, since it encompasses her early life, her history-making space walk, and, of course, her work developing and launching the groundbreaking Hubble Space Telescope. Shannon Lucid wrote a book of her own, called *Tumbleweed*, which chronicles her training and experience living aboard the Mir space station for six months—a highlight of her career that, unfortunately, didn't fall within the arc of my book. I highly recommend these books to those who want to go deeper into the struggles—and triumphs—of the Six.

Those looking for a detailed portrait of the life of Sally Ride won't find a better one than Lynn Sherr's tremendous *Sally Ride: America's First Woman in Space*. Lynn provides a vibrant history of a woman who was notoriously private during her time on Earth, and Lynn's intrepid reporting served as an essential launching point for my book. *Sally Ride* is especially informative about Sally's storied career after leaving NASA. As Lynn and Tam point out, Sally's work as an astronaut only encompassed nine years of her life; there's much more to Sally's tale than flying to space.

Since Judy Resnik was such a private person, detailed accounts of her life are relatively scarce. However, there are a few remarkable texts I relied on to get insight into her personality and career. *Esquire* published a feature on Judy with input from her father and mother, and one of the authors of that article, Christine Spolar, wrote a chapter on Judy for the *Washington Post*'s book on the *Challenger* tragedy, which honored the lives of the astronauts.

Additionally, astronaut Mike Mullane, who flew with Judy on STS-41-D, wrote a hilarious and engaging memoir chronicling his time at NASA called *Riding Rockets*, in which he recounts his relationship with Judy. I turned to that book for reference several times in writing my own.

Since my book was focused on the Six, I didn't go into as much detail as I could have on the thirteen women who passed Randy Lovelace's astronaut tests. For that history, I turned to Margaret Weitekamp and her extraordinary book, *Right Stuff, Wrong Sex*, an extremely well-researched text on the history of these women and their fight to fly to space. That book goes into even greater depth on Jackie Cochran and her involvement in both starting the program and contributing to its demise. I very much recommend it if you're looking to learn about this era.

Other texts and content I greatly relied on include Michael Cassutt's *The Astronaut Maker*, a riveting in-depth portrait of George Abbey, and David Shayler and Colin Burgess's *NASA's First Space Shuttle Astronaut Selection*, which provides a vivid account of the entire TFNG class and their integration into NASA. In writing this book I was also fortunate to be able to consult *The Real Stuff*, *Wings in Orbit*, *The Challenger Launch Decision*, *The Burning Blue*, and Netflix's *Challenger: The Final Flight* docuseries. A full list of my sourcing for *The Six—Young Readers Edition* can be found on my website, lorengrush.com.

ACKNOWLEDGMENTS

This book wouldn't have been possible without the open and thoughtful help of so many people. Above all, I want to thank the still-living members of the Six who participated in this project when they were able and who directed me to various sources to help tell their stories. They graciously endured my countless emails and phone calls, and the stories they shared with me and others over the years made this a dream project to work on.

I also want to thank the Six's former colleagues, notably their fellow TFNG classmates, many of whom sat with me for hours, divulging their life stories in great detail. For a few brief moments in interviews, I felt as if I was a fly on the wall during TFNG training. I want to especially thank Hoot Gibson, Steve Hawley, John Fabian, and Rick Hauck, who spoke with me for far too many hours and provided vivid and absorbing details. But I'm immensely thankful for every person who agreed to speak with me for this book.

I'm hugely grateful to Tam O'Shaughnessy for sharing with me her memories of Sally's life and providing key documents and recordings from Sally's time at NASA.

Thanks, also, to those at NASA who guided me to the right people and sourcing I needed, especially Jennifer Ross-Nazzal, Brandi Dean, Brian Odom, Robert Young, and Holly McIntyre.

A big shout-out to Paul—whose last name I do not know—at the New York Public Library. When I set out to write a book during the height of COVID-19, I naively thought it would be easy since I'd have all the time at home to work on it. But I soon learned the difficulties of trying to conduct research when every major archive in the United States was closed. Over Zoom, Paul, a researcher at the library, patiently spent hours walking me through the labyrinthian online archival system, and, thanks to his help, I was able to pull a significant amount of information without leaving my home.

I'd be nothing without the NASA chroniclers who came before me and who shared with me their insight, including Lynn Sherr, Michael Cassutt, Dave Shayler, and Stephen Slater. I only hope that my work is half as good as the stories they've told and the work they've collected over the years.

Special thanks are reserved for Robert Pearlman, who served as my space historian guide throughout this process and provided valuable advice, sourcing, and fact-checking. I'm forever in your debt and unendingly appreciative that you took all my calls.

I'm also grateful to Christine Spolar and Scott Spencer, who happily delved back into their reporting and memories from nearly thirty years ago. Thanks as well to Ryan Millager for helping to open up the past for me.

To have the time to write and focus on this book, my two successive employers—*The Verge* and Bloomberg—graciously gave me the time I needed to step away from full-time reporting. Not everyone has that luxury, and I consider myself very fortunate to have had that time. I also want to highlight my time at *The Verge*, a place that made me the reporter I am today and gave me the skill set I needed to write this book. My seven years there were life-changing.

To Rick Horgan, my editor, thank you for understanding the story I wanted to tell with this book and for providing the platform to do so. Together, I truly believe we've crafted something special. Susan Canavan, thank you for plucking me out of obscurity back in 2020 and taking a chance on me. You really are my fairy godmother, and you have helped change my life.

To Stephan, my mentor, there are simply not enough thank-yous to cover the amount of guidance and advice you have given me. At first, writing this book felt like wandering down a pitch-black hallway, but with your help, a light finally turned on.

Before I delved into space history, I was first and foremost a space reporter, and I've had the privilege of working alongside a truly outstanding peer group of space journalists who are the most supportive and gifted people I know. Only a tiny fraction of the population knows what it's like to do what we do, and I feel so honored to be part of this special group.

To my friends, thank you for your unwavering support and for putting up with my prolonged absences on nights and weekends. Lea, Dan, and Hayley, thank you for helping me navigate the moving-picture world. And Christina, above all, I love you, and I'm so happy to have your shoulder to lean on.

Space is in my blood thanks to my parents, Gene and Joyce Grush, who both worked for decades on the space shuttle program at Johnson Space Center. I want to thank them for bringing me into this world—both the Earth world and the space world—and for supporting me in all my absurd endeavors. I truly had a fantastic launchpad and I love you both so much.

And, of course, I want to thank my crewmate, Chris. I could write another book filled with all the support and guidance you've given me during our years together. There's no one I'd rather explore this universe with.